The Lovehandles

Photos on the front and back covers were taken by Ed Vidinghoff and appeared in the article "Weekend Rockers" written by Pam Brinkley for the Oregonian's Northwest Magazine, Sunday, February 23, 1986. On the front cover (from left) are Tom Hoggard, Les Naman, Patti Dunahugh, Mike Bragg, Bob Crumpacker, and Bart McMullan. Soundman Warner Swarner's head is visible just below the first "L." On the back cover, top row, are Bob Crumpacker and Warner Swarner, middle row, Patti Dunahugh, Les Naman, Tom Hoggard, and Bart McMullan, bottom row, Mike Bragg.

Layout/Design by Gail Watson,
Resolute Printing, Newberg, Oregon

The Lovehandles

Independently Published by
Robert Crumpacker

To Bands Everywhere

TABLE OF CONTENTS

INTRODUCTION i
CONFESSION iii

Chapter 1: PATTI'S LAST STAND 1

Chapter 2: ME 7
    The New Music 11
    I Get Serious 13
    Portland, Oregon 14
    Portland Adventist Hospital 17
    The Invitation. 24

Chapter 3: TOM 27

Chapter 4: HOUSES 37
    What The. . . ? 39

Chapter 5: LARRY FRANKS 43

Chapter 6: BART 49

Chapter 7: PATTI 67

Chapter 8: THE BAND TAKES OFF 71
    The Kuehnel's Party. 72
    Johnny Limbo and the Lugnuts 74
    Franks Talks Dirty. 75
    Caroline, Tim, and Bill 78
    Love Machine? 79
    The Samples' New Year's Eve Party 80
    Names 82

Chapter 9: LES 85

Chapter 10: ROMANCE 95
    The Engagement 97
    Mount Saint Helens   99
    Our Soundtrack 100
    The Wedding 101

Chapter 11: AFTER THE WEDDING 105
    Music and Electronics 106
    Band Practice 109
    A Joyous Noise?   110
    Dance 113
    Anatomy of a Party 114
    The Great Facilitator 115
    Angel's Gig 118
    Set List For Angel's Party 120
    Bowman's 121
    Dreams 122

PICTURES *125-134*

Chapter 12: MIKE 135
    Mike Bragg 136

Chapter 13: THE NEARLY FORGOTTEN YEARS (1982-1984) . . 149
    Angel's II 150
    Samples' II 150
    The Oregon Yacht Club 150
    Navy League Dance, Masonic Hall 151

Chapter 14: ANDY 157

Chapter 15: GAINING TRACTION (1985 to 1986) 161

OMPRO Set List 162
The Great Hall 164
The Bat Mitzvah 166
Larry Franks Again 166
The Franks' Valentine's Day Party 168
The Gigs Keep Coming 174
The Irvington Club 175
Rose City Sound and Lighting 176

Chapter 16: THE BIG PROBLEM 179
Mike's Dilemma 180
The Columbia Gorge Hotel and Spa 183
The Announcement 186
Patti Struggles 189
And the Band Plays On 191
The April Fool's Day Dance 192
April Fool's Day Dance Set List 193
Kaiser Permanente Dance (Cancelled) 195
Bart Says It All 196

Chapter 17: THE BEAT GOES ON 199

Chapter 18: EPILOGUE
Patti 205
Tom 209
Bart 213
Larry Franks 221
Andy 222
Me 224
Les 231
Mike 233

ACKNOWLEDGEMENTS 237
POSTSCRIPT 238

INTRODUCTION

Several years ago, my friend Scott Huff told me a story about his father, Charlie, who was a navigator during World War II. Like many soldiers of that era who were sent to do jobs that they weren't really qualified to do, Charlie had a problem that should have disqualified him from becoming a navigator: he had trouble thinking spatially. I'm not sure what the name for this condition is, but it must have been rare enough to escape detection on the many tests that Charlie took before becoming a navigator. In fact, he may not have known about it until he first sat in the navigator's seat of a B-24 bomber.

Specifically, Charlie had a problem working with angles that prevented him from plotting a navigational course from where he was to where he was supposed to go, which of course is the primary function of a navigator. But he was able to plot a course in reverse—that is, from his destination to his location—and in most situations that worked well enough.

But of course it didn't always work. Navigators not suffering from Lieutenant Huff's condition could work a navigational problem from where they were to where they wanted to go, which became important when you were lost. But unfortunately Lieutenant Huff wasn't able to do this, and when his plane became separated from their squadron on a run from Brazil to North Africa, he needed help from his crew to plot a new course. But otherwise, Lieutenant Huff performed admirably, proving that even in navigation you don't have to be perfect to be effective—a concept that applies equally well to the subject of this book.

I played in a band called the Lovehandles in and around Portland, Oregon, between 1979 and 1989. None of its members were full-time musicians. Patti Dunahugh, our female vocalist, was a dental hygienist;

Mike Bragg, our male vocalist and rhythm guitarist, was a medical statistician; and the rest of us were doctors. Of the six of us, the only one whose level of talent qualified him for the designation of "real musician" was Mike.

But despite Mike's presence and our best efforts, we were not a great band. In fact, we weren't even a good band, and the discrepancy between the quality of our music and the success that we enjoyed has always puzzled me. But whatever the reason, we proved repeatedly that you don't have to be perfect to please people. And much like Charlie in the navigator's seat of his B-24, most of the time we got you where you wanted to go.

The impetus for this book was Patti Dunahugh's death, which hit me much harder than I expected. After Tom Hoggard and I, Patti was the third person in the band, and was our singer from 1979 until 1982, when Mike Bragg joined the band and shared the vocals. But as you will see, Patti was much more than our singer, and had it not been for her grit and determination the band would likely have folded after its second gig.

Although it's bad enough that we all have to die, it's even worse that most of us will have no idea when that's going to happen, because if we did, we could spend some time thanking all the people who made our lives better before kicking our respective buckets. But that's not the way it works.

The first member of the band to go was our keyboard player, Les Naman, who died unexpectedly in 2014. Of course, his death came as a shock, but after commiserating with one another and feeling vulnerable for a while, we went back to assuming that the rest of us were made of sterner stuff. But when Patti died, it became impossible to believe that we were anything but mortal, which meant that if I didn't say what I had to say, it would never get said.

Although it's too late to tell Les and Patti that their lives were important to me, this book is my way of thanking the band's remaining members—Tom, Bart, and Mike—for the happiness the band brought me. Thanks, guys. It was a blast.

CONFESSION

I'm not a writer. I'm trying to become one, but I'm not quite there, and probably never will be. I'm afraid that I've come to writing too late in life to ever attain the status of "real writer," so for the sake of accuracy I'll refer to myself as a would-be writer. But as a would-be writer, I face the same challenges that real writers encounter when trying to write a book of this type: an account of something that actually happened. Of course, many things that actually happen—geologic events, astronomical events, and the life cycle of the butterfly—don't involve people, or if they do, they involve them in such a peripheral way that in-depth characterizations are unnecessary. But books about bands rely heavily on the people involved. So, one of the challenges that a writer—real or otherwise—faces when writing about a band is getting the people right, which not only involves telling what happened and how it happened, but also who was responsible for making it happen, and what personal qualities enabled them to make it happen. And since I'm not a real writer, all I can say is that I've done my best.

CHAPTER 1: PATTI'S LAST STAND

On Sunday, May 7, 2017, Mike Bragg called to tell me that Patti Dunahugh had died. He said that his wife had read it on Facebook. News of Patti's death hit me with equal parts disbelief and sadness. Disbelief because Patty was so stubborn that it was hard to picture her succumbing to anything, death included, and sadness because many years before, Mike, myself, and three other men had shared something very precious with Patti: a band by the name of the Lovehandles.

My first call was to Patti's husband, Bart McMullan. Bart would be devastated, and I wanted to be helpful to him in any way I could. Bart was a retired physician who had made the decision during his previous marriage not to have children; he would find his happiness elsewhere. And as it turned out, he did. With Patti, her daughter Amy, his medical career, their home, their friends, and a dog or two, he had more than enough to make him happy.

Although Bart's first words to me were so choked with grief that they were barely intelligible, he was eventually able to relate the essential features of the last two days. He began by saying that for the past three years they had known that Patti had a small aortic aneurysm.

An aneurysm is an area of enlargement on the wall of an artery caused by a weakening of the artery's wall. It is much like the bubbles that can appear on the wall of an old inner tube. Although Patti's aneurysm was small—less than two inches long—the aorta is the largest and most important blood vessel in the body, carrying oxygen-rich blood to the heart, the head, the arms, and everything else, down to and including the legs. Although anything wrong with the aorta must be viewed with concern, less than two weeks before her death Patti had undergone a CT angiogram, a test which confirmed that the aneurysm

1

hadn't changed since it was first detected, which, of course, was very good news.

I should also tell you that an aneurysm can develop anywhere along the course of the aorta, but those in the chest, especially those near the heart, are by far the most dangerous, and that, unfortunately, was the location of Patti's aneurysm.

On the morning of Saturday, May 6, one day before her death, Patti developed chest pain, so Bart drove her to the emergency room of Portland, Oregon's Providence St. Vincent Medical Center. Although her pain could have come from any number of sources, the first thing that Bart thought of was the aneurysm. But shortly after arriving in the ER, Patti's pain improved, and when her blood pressure was taken and an electrocardiogram was done, both tests were normal. Then the ER physician ordered a number of blood tests, and those, too, were normal.

Bart and the ER doctor discussed the possibility that her pain could have come from a sudden enlargement of the aneurysm, but Patti's recent CT angiogram, her normal tests, and the fact that she was feeling better seemed to argue against it. Although Patti's aneurysm was still front and center in Bart's thinking, he decided not to push for another CT angiogram.

Then Patti further discouraged the idea by announcing that she knew exactly what her pain was due to—it was due to acid reflux. Patti had been bothered by acid reflux in the past, and she now insisted that the pain she felt with acid reflux was exactly the same pain she had felt at home. And because she had always treated this by taking half a teaspoon of sodium bicarbonate—common baking soda—in water every two hours until her symptoms disappeared, she would prove to everyone that she was right by treating her remaining discomfort with baking soda, and she instructed the doctor to order some sodium bicarbonate from the pharmacy.

When the doctor explained that giving sodium bicarbonate was not the hospital's accepted means for treating acid reflux—and therefore was not available from the pharmacy—Patti was outraged.

"Then go to the kitchen and get me some baking soda," she told him.

The doctor did his best to explain that going to the kitchen for baking soda would be equally impossible, but instead of baking soda he would be happy to prescribe the hospital's preferred method of treating acid reflux—a mixture of medicines called the "GI cocktail."

Patti wouldn't hear of it. She wanted baking soda.

Then Bart stepped into the fray by telling her, "Damn it, Patti, just try the GI cocktail, please . . ."

But Patti, who could be one of the world's most stubborn women, would have baking soda or nothing.

At that point, the ER doctor suggested that because all of her tests had been normal and she was feeling better, she might consider going home. If her symptoms returned, she could always come back. That seemed acceptable to everyone, and Patti was discharged with a diagnosis of "indigestion."

Patty slept well overnight, but the following morning the pain returned, and this time it was worse than it had been the day before. And in addition to the pain, this time Patti actually looked sick—something she hadn't the day before. She was sweaty and pale, and when Bart took her blood pressure, it was elevated. Now more concerned than ever, they threw on some clothes, rushed out to the car, and arrived at the ER around 8:15 a.m. But just as had happened the day before, upon reaching the hospital her pain improved.

Patti was met at the front desk by the triage nurse, whose job it was to screen patients according to the severity of their symptoms. The nurse asked her the nature of her problem, and Patti, who at that moment was feeling well enough to smile, did so and said "chest pain."

But afraid that Patti was now minimizing her symptoms, Bart told the nurse, "Her pain was much worse at home. She was pale and clammy, and her blood pressure was elevated."

But looking unconvinced, the nurse took Patti's blood pressure and performed another electrocardiogram, and when both were normal, Patti was told to take a seat in the waiting room—the implication being that she wasn't sick enough to be seen right away by a doctor.

THE LOVEHANDLES

Although Patti felt better than she had at home, she was by no means comfortable, and their time in the waiting room ticked by with agonizing slowness. After an hour, Patti wanted to go home, but Bart, who was still worried about the aneurysm, convinced her to stay.

Finally, around 9:45 a.m., Patti's name was called, and they were led into a small examination room. Then a nurse entered, drew some blood, and left.

Although the blood that the nurse had just drawn was largely for the same tests that had been done the day before, one test was different. This was a D-dimer test, which became abnormal when a blood clot or blood clots formed anywhere within the body. Although it was most commonly used to identify blood clots in the lungs, a condition known as pulmonary embolism, it could detect blood clots anywhere, including blood that was trapped within the wall of an enlarging aneurysm.

After the blood draw, they sat in the exam room for an hour or more before a young woman burst into the room and identified herself as the emergency room doctor. She said that she had read Patti's records from the day before, the D-dimer test that she had ordered was abnormal, and she recommended that Patty undergo a CT angiogram—immediately.

Although Patti's situation was now worrisome, another worrisome situation had been on Bart and Patti's minds since they arrived in the ER: they had left home without letting their dog, Sulay, outside for her morning ritual. With that in mind, Bart asked how long the CT angiogram would take. The doctor estimated an hour, which would give Bart enough time to drive home and take care of Sulay. So as Patti was wheeled off to the radiology department, Bart left to attend to their dog.

Bart made the round trip in forty-five minutes, just minutes before Patti returned from the CT angiogram. Then the ER doctor rushed into the room looking worried. The aneurysm, she said, had changed: it had grown larger and was leaking blood into the wall of the aorta as well as into the pericardium, the membranous sack surrounding the heart. This condition of blood surrounding the heart was called cardiac tamponade (pronounced "tam-puh-NOD"), and was particularly dangerous because blood in the pericardium can compress the heart, impairing its ability to pump blood.

Now Patti's condition was a real emergency, and if she were going to survive, she would need surgery as soon as possible. But surgery to fix an aneurysm near the heart is a very specialized procedure that only a cardiac surgery team can perform. Although St. Vincent's had such a team, when the ER physician asked them to see Patti, they were involved with another case and would not be available for hours. A team from some other hospital would need to be found. More calls were made, and the cardiac surgery team at Portland's Oregon Health and Science University—OHSU—was available. Patti was rushed there by ambulance, but she worsened on the way and was pronounced dead in the OHSU emergency room.

A CT angiogram is neither dangerous nor particularly invasive. It requires that a dye be injected into the bloodstream while a specialized type of x-ray machine takes some pictures—nothing more. Although Patti's life might have been saved if a CT angiogram had been done on the first, or even early on the second day of their visits to the ER, the CT angiogram she had had less than two weeks before made another seem unnecessary.

But a good case can be made for thinking that Patti's death, tragic though it was, may have been for the best. The main risk associated with an aneurysm of the aortic arch—and surgery done to fix it—is damaging one or more of the three blood vessels that leave the top of the arch and go to the brain, causing a stroke. And for Patti, that would have been worse than death.

CHAPTER 2: ME

Late in my mother's pregnancy, my parents drove from Rochester, Minnesota, where my father was a surgical resident at the Mayo Clinic, to Peru, Illinois—350 miles—to visit my mother's parents one last time before her delivery. But in Peru, my father developed abdominal pain, and thinking that he might have appendicitis, asked my mother to drive him back to Rochester. But on the way his condition deteriorated, and by the time they reached the Mayo Clinic, my father was critically ill.

At first the cause of his illness was unknown, but an observant physician noticed that when my father's temperature increased, his pulse rate decreased—just the opposite of what usually happened. This unusual combination of temperature and pulse was known as Faget's sign (after Jean Charles Faget, the Louisiana physician who first described it) and it was characteristic of a handful of infectious diseases, typhoid fever among them. Today typhoid fever can be treated with antibiotics, but back then antibiotics didn't exist. So when additional tests confirmed that my father had typhoid fever, if he were going to recover, he would have to do so on his own.

My father fell into a coma, and during that time, my mother went into labor. I was born on January 17, 1941. Then, to everyone's surprise, my father began to improve, and continued improving until he could look out his hospital window and see my mother holding me up for his inspection. Unfortunately, the excitement from this caused him to relapse, but then he rallied once more—this time for good—and was able to complete his surgical training.

By then the United States had entered World War II, and although my father wanted to serve as a military surgeon, the typhoid fever had classified him as 4-F: unfit for military service. But the upside of his situation was that doctors throughout the country were being drafted in wholesale quantities, creating practice opportunities for those who, like my father, were ineligible for the draft.

My father had decided that he wanted to live near my mother's parents in Illinois rather than return to his native Kansas, and he was delighted to hear that a medical clinic in Champaign, Illinois, had lost one of its surgeons to the war effort and was looking for another. My father applied, was offered the job, and accepted.

This turned out to be a mistake. Despite my father's training at the prestigious Mayo Clinic, all that the surgeons at the clinic in Champaign wanted was someone to evaluate their patients pre-operatively, assist during their surgeries, and care for them post-operatively—in other words, they wanted a surgical flunky. My father stayed for the duration of his contract (one year) and then quit. We moved again, this time to Wichita, Kansas, a city of 115 thousand, just sixty miles south of the farm where my father had been raised.

As far back as my memory will reach, I remember my mother playing the piano. Although she knew a broad assortment of music, the songs of Stephen Foster and the popular music of her youth were her favorites. Of these, she loved "Body and Soul" the most, playing it so beautifully that I never tired of hearing it.

Our first phonograph was an old upright Victrola that had to be cranked by hand before it would play. Our collection of records was large and diverse: children's stories about Piccolo Pete and Jack and the Beanstalk, the novelty recordings of Spike Jones, a fictitious farting contest between Paul Boomer and Lord Windesmere, and a number of classical recordings, including the music of Enrico Caruso. I loved them all.

In kindergarten, my teacher would play the piano and sing while we beat along with sand blocks and sticks, a few tambourines, a couple of triangles, a pair of cymbals, and a drum. Although I always raised my hand when the teacher asked who wanted to play the drum, I was always given the sand blocks or sticks.

I couldn't sing. Despite encouragement from my teachers, I could never carry a tune, and by the third grade I was assigned a place in the last row of the school chorus and told to just move my lips.

In grade school I took piano lessons from old Mr. Scott, a former patient of my father's whose eyesight was so bad that he wore a second pair of glasses taped on top of the first. Although I would have loved to play the piano like my mother, the process of transforming the tiny black dots on the pages of John Thompson's "Teaching Little Fingers to Play" into listenable music seemed beyond my ability. But I struggled on until my first recital when I played a song about a bumblebee so poorly that I would never play the piano again.

A few years later, my parents convinced me to take clarinet lessons from a man who had once played with John Philip Sousa, but my progress was slow, my interest waned, and like the piano, the clarinet became history.

But when I was in the sixth grade I heard a recording of the Benny Goodman Orchestra's famous 1938 Carnegie Hall concert with Gene Krupa on the drums, and for the first time in my life I actually wanted to play a musical instrument. I wanted to play the drums.

But my parents were hesitant. By then they had nothing to show for the money they had already spent on my musical efforts, and they wanted some guarantee that I would stick with another musical instrument before buying something as expensive as a set of drums. So we struck a deal. They would get me an inexpensive snare drum, and if I were still playing it after one year, they would buy me a drum kit.

That night my father and I drove to the Wichita Music Company, where he bought me a cheap snare drum, a wobbly drum stand, and a couple of pairs of sticks—all for twenty dollars. Returning home, I set the drum in front of our Scott radio/phonograph, put Benny Goodman's "Sing, Sing, Sing" on the turntable, and magically transformed into Gene Krupa crouched behind his massive Slingerland drum kit, creating irresistible rhythms and sending the Carnegie Hall crowd (especially the women) into orgasmic frenzies.

THE LOVEHANDLES

For a year I beat that poor drum mercilessly. Then one Sunday morning as our family was sitting around the breakfast table eating pancakes and reading the funny papers, my dad mentioned that there was an ad in the paper for a used set of drums. Did I think we should take a look at them?

I was both excited and frightened. Although a set of drums was exactly what I wanted, a real drum kit would mean trading my hugely successful performances in front of the Scott for real performances in front of real people, however embarrassing those might be. For unlike the handsome and charismatic Krupa, I was big, awkward, and shy. But still I wanted to try. I had to try. So I nodded my head and said yes, I would like to see those drums.

So after breakfast, my dad and I climbed into our family's Buick Roadmaster—in those days, doctors were expected to drive Buicks—and drove to a neighborhood where shabby houses and grimy commercial buildings conjured visions of crime and depravity that only added to my discomfort. My father found the address, pulled into the parking lot of a small motel, and knocked on one of the doors until it was opened by a young man who looked like he had just rolled out of bed.

But behind him, in the middle of the room, was the most beautiful set of drums I had ever seen. It was a full kit: a chrome-backed drummer's throne surrounded by a black snare, a black bass drum, two black tom-toms, and a generous complement of cymbals. I glanced at my father and could see that even he was impressed. My dad asked the young man why he was selling his drums, and we were told that although he had come to town as part of a band, the band members had argued, the band had broken up, and now he needed to sell his drums to get back home.

I looked more closely at his kit and saw that the drums were all Slingerlands and the cymbals were all Zildjians, just like those of the great Gene Krupa. My father asked how much he wanted for everything, and the young man said two hundred dollars—a lot of money in those days. My dad considered this, then asked me if I liked them. Yes, I said, very much, and without contesting the price, my dad reached into his wallet and counted out two hundred dollars. The young man helped us load them into our car, my father wished him well, and we drove back home.

The short version of a long story is that I never became a great drummer, or even a very good drummer, but my love affair with the drums never ended. I took one drum lesson, didn't like the teacher, and quit—in retrospect, a terrible mistake. And though my lack of training meant that most of the local drummers were technically superior to me, none were more enthusiastic, and despite my limitations I managed to play with a handful of bands.

The first gig I ever played was a school dance in a junior high gymnasium. My friend Frank Lygrisse played the trumpet and another kid played the piano. Regardless of the song's initial speed, I gradually increased the tempo until we were playing it as fast as we could, and then I ended the song with an extended drum solo, which sounded just awesome echoing throughout the gym. We were a big hit, especially with the girls, who came by during our breaks to beg us to keep playing.

The New Music

My junior high bands played a mixture of Dixieland jazz, country and western, and music from the big band era. Dixieland classics like "When the Saints Go Marching In" and "Muskrat Ramble" were our fast songs, while romantic numbers like "Tennessee Waltz," "Tenderly," and "Stardust" were our slow songs. But things were about to change.

In the summer of 1955, before my sophomore year of high school, my parents sent me to a summer camp in Minnesota named Camp Lincoln. The campers were from all over the country, but the most interesting group was from Oklahoma City, their leader a little kid named Johnny Franklin who looked like he'd never spent a day in the great outdoors.

Although the rest of us came to camp wearing sneakers and sporting crew cuts, Johnny arrived in black wingtips, his dark hair meticulously slicked back into a ducktail. Most of us had brought sports equipment—

footballs, baseballs, baseball gloves—but not Johnny. Sports weren't really his thing. Instead, Johnny had brought a little record player and a stack of forty-five-rpm records, which spoke a language more universal than sports. For as much as we loved sports, I think I can safely say that we were more interested in sex, and Johnny was there to deliver that part of the camp experience.

Although all of Johnny's records had their merits, the ones we listened to the most were by Hank Ballard and the Midnighters, who performed songs like "Get It," "Sexy Ways," "Work with Me, Annie," and "Annie Had a Baby" with a rawness and an honesty that we had never heard before. And to enhance the band's credibility, Johnny said that the Federal Communications Commission considered their music so objectionable that it had been banned from the airways—and what could be a finer recommendation than that?

Then one night Johnny put on "Work with Me, Annie," and began dancing a slow, sinuous dance with a rhythmic back-and-forth movement of his hips that he called the "bop," and followed that with a performance of the even more salacious "dirty bop." We were in heaven.

Camp that year was the best of both worlds. During the day we were outside in the fresh air, wholesomely swimming, canoeing, and riding horses, while at night we were dancing the dirty bop to Hank Ballard and the Midnighters.

Johnny's records were a revelation. Although we had been hearing music about love since we were born, there was another step in the male-female dynamic that no one had sung about, and that was sex. And while we weren't sure whether sex led to love or love led to sex, we knew that sex was the key. Love was something that you felt, something that came to you passively, but sex was an active process. You fell in love, but you *performed* sex, and how that was done was the mystery that we needed to solve.

Returning home from camp, it was as though Johnny's music had opened my ears, and I was suddenly aware of how popular music was changing. There was now a mixture of old and new music coming over the airways, with much of the new music addressing subjects that we teenagers were most curious about—fast cars, drinking, and sex—and this was being delivered in a new musical style called rock and roll.

I Get Serious

I played my drums in high school and even took them with me to college, but once I began thinking about a "real career," I packed them away.

The family business was medicine. My maternal grandfather had been a general practitioner, and my father was a general surgeon. My mother had worked at the Mayo Clinic, and my sister, Nancy, would eventually become an oncologist. Dinnertime at our house was filled with accounts of my father's medical adventures, replete with all their gory details. Although I tried to break from this tradition, medicine was in my blood, and I finally applied to the University of Kansas (KU) School of Medicine and was accepted.

Midway through my final year of medical school, we seniors were expected to pick the location for the next phase of our medical training: the internship. Internships were one-year programs designed to give recent medical school graduates some practical, hands-on experience, and they could be done at any one of hundreds of hospitals throughout the United States. To assist in our selection, representatives from many of these hospitals would be visiting KU in the hope of attracting us to their programs.

KU also kept records of where its graduates had gone in previous years, which I looked through as I tried to make my decision. Although most had gone to Midwestern hospitals, I noticed that each year somewhere between five and ten KU graduates interned at Oregon hospitals—most often at hospitals associated with the University of Oregon or at a private hospital in Portland named Good Samaritan. I had no idea why so many KU grads picked Oregon, but the idea of going somewhere new and different was attractive, and I thought I'd look into it.

The Lovehandles

When I checked the list of hospital representatives scheduled to visit KU, I saw that in a few days Dr. Spence Meaghan, the medical director of Portland's Good Samaritan Hospital, would be there to speak with interested seniors.

I met with Dr. Meaghan and listened to his pitch. I liked him and liked his program. He told me that Dr. Robert Dow, one of the country's premier neurologists, practiced at Good Samaritan and that as an intern I could rotate through his service. That was particularly attractive to me, because earlier that year I had taken a neurology elective and enjoyed it so much that I was considering neurology as a career. To sweeten the deal, Good Samaritan would pay for my airfare, so with nothing to lose, I decided to go.

Portland, Oregon

The dust, heat, and flat, featureless topography of Kansas did not prepare me for Oregon. Nearing the end of our four-hour flight, the plane descended through a dense cloudbank and suddenly an immense snow-covered mountain was drifting by us on our left, while hills and forests of the deepest green unrolled beneath us. It was like nothing I had ever seen.

My ground-level contact with Portland was equally intriguing. It was the winter of 1968, only a few months removed from San Francisco's Summer of Love, and Portland was in the midst of the same cultural revolution as its Californian counterpart. Flashing peace signs, long-haired young men thumbed for rides on city streets while braless young women sold handmade candles, pottery, and leather goods in patchouli-scented shops. Record stores, their walls covered with posters urging us to "Make Love, Not War" and proclaiming "Power to the People," blasted out the trippy, psychedelic music of Jimi Hendrix, Janis Joplin, and the Grateful Dead. Nothing like this was happening in Kansas, and I was more than a little intrigued.

Then there were Oregon's outdoor activities: three ski areas were one hour to the east, ocean fishing and crabbing were one hour to the west, and boating and waterskiing were on the nearby Columbia and Willamette Rivers.

Even Good Samaritan Hospital did not disappoint: it was modern, well equipped, and welcoming. The staff physicians, interns, and residents were helpful and friendly. I talked with Dr. Robert Dow, who answered my questions and introduced me to his interns and residents. Everyone seemed happy and anxious to please, and by the time I was back in Kansas City, I had decided to intern at Good Samaritan in Portland.

My internship year was one of the best of my life. Not only was I able to rotate through two months of neurology and two months of neurosurgery, but I also learned to ski, went ocean fishing, climbed a ten thousand-foot mountain, and saw the Steve Miller Band and the Grateful Dead in concert, stoned.

The only problem was my marriage. My wife and I had married after my senior year of medical school, and when we met a few months before that, it had seemed like we were perfectly matched: we were both from Kansas and both had been English majors in college. In addition, Mary was smart, attractive, and unattached, so after a handful of dates I asked her to marry me.

Although I didn't know it then, marriage during the final year of medical school can be risky. The reason for this is sometimes referred to as "senior year insecurity," which means that approaching graduation without a life partner can sometimes create a desire to find one before facing the world alone. The trick, of course, is choosing the right life partner.

In retrospect, had we taken more time to get to know each other, we probably wouldn't have married. But that didn't happen. And though I'm sure there was much about my internship year that my wife enjoyed, too, at its conclusion there could be little doubt that our marriage was in trouble.

Following my internship, I began the final phase of my medical training: a neurology residency at the University of Minnesota in

Minneapolis. Although this was a three-year program, I would be leaving Minnesota after my first year to enter the Army. The reason for this was the war in Vietnam and something called the Berry Plan.

In 1968, deployment for the Vietnam War was at its peak, and many of the country's young men—doctors included—were being drafted. To insure that there were enough doctors to care for its troops and their families, the Department of Defense was offering young physicians something called the Berry Plan. Signing up for this program ensured that you knew when you would be serving your two-year commitment so that you could plan around it. The other option was to forgo the Berry Plan and risk being drafted at a very inconvenient time, like after buying a home and starting your medical practice. Since most young doctors wanted as much control over their futures as possible, the majority considered the Berry Plan the better choice.

When I signed up for the Berry Plan, the Department of Defense informed me that after one year of neurology training, I would be serving my two years in the Army. I was lucky. Those who entered the service either after their internships or after their residencies usually wound up in Vietnam, but doctors with one year of training more often stayed stateside and practiced their specialties. So after one year at the University of Minnesota, I was sent to Darnall Army Medical Center at Fort Hood, Texas, to become its new chief of neurology. If you think that becoming chief of neurology of a large hospital after only one year of neurology training is a bit inappropriate, well, I did, too. But that was the way it worked.

I stayed at Fort Hood both years, and during the second year my wife and I separated. I served out the remainder of my Army obligation, then returned to Minneapolis and completed the last two years of my residency. At that point, my medical education was complete, and it was time to choose where I would live and practice medicine—perhaps for the rest of my life. I chose Portland.

But before moving to Portland, I had to find a neurology practice that was both looking for a neurologist and would agree to have me. So

I contacted Kirby Griffin, one of the internal medicine residents I had met during my year at Good Samaritan, and asked him to check out practice opportunities in Portland. A few weeks later Kirby called to say that after contacting every neurology office in the city, he had found that Dr. David Rich, a neurologist working at Providence Hospital on the east side of town, was looking for a partner. I called Dr. Rich, and he agreed to meet with me. I flew to Portland and we hit it off. He offered me a job, and I accepted.

Portland Adventist Hospital

Becoming successful in private practice is all about networking, and as Portland's newest neurologist it was important for me to make myself known to the other doctors on the east side of town. So besides working at Providence Hospital, I began consulting at all the other east-side hospitals, and though this involved a lot of driving, it was absolutely critical to my success.

Then something unexpected happened. Of all the hospitals that I was consulting at, there was one that I enjoyed more than Providence. Its name was Portland Adventist Hospital.

Most medical specialists get their patients by way of referral from other doctors. This is especially true of neurologists, who advertise themselves as seeing patients "by referral only." Although we are happy to get patients from anyone, most of our patients come from primary care providers—in other words, from general practitioners, family physicians, and internal medicine specialists (internists).

To the layperson, the differences between these three can be confusing, so I'll explain them. Prior to 1969, all doctors were divided into general practitioners and specialists, but in 1969 a new specialty called "family practice" was established. Initially, all general practitioners were folded into this new designation, but in 1995 the American Board of General Practice was founded, and the two were separated.

But despite their separation, the differences between family practitioners and general practitioners are minor. Although family practitioners consider themselves specialists and general practitioners don't, both care for adults and children, both deliver babies, and both perform a limited number of surgeries. Internists, on the other hand, receive no obstetrical or surgical training and do not care for children.

Since internists spend no time learning how to deliver babies, perform surgery, or care for kids, they spend more time learning about the various medical subspecialties, including neurology. This means that internists have a better grasp of neurology than general practitioners or family practitioners, and from a neurologist's standpoint, that has one very practical consequence: you will get more patients from general practitioners and family practitioners than you will from internists.

From that standpoint, Providence Hospital and Portland Adventist Hospital were very different. Besides being a much larger hospital than Adventist, internists did most of Providence's primary care, while general practitioners and family practitioners did the lion's share of Adventist's primary care. And although Providence had Dave Rich, Adventist had no full-time neurologist and needed one badly.

In addition to feeling more appreciated at Adventist than I was at Providence, Adventist was in the midst of a huge expansion project. Although I had been seeing patients at the old Portland Adventist Hospital on Southeast 60th Avenue and Belmont Street, ground had already been broken for the new Adventist Medical Center on Southeast 100th Avenue and Market Street. And because this new facility would be much larger than the old one, Adventist was actively looking for a number of additional doctors, including a full-time neurologist.

I wasn't unhappy at Providence. I liked Dave Rich. He was a good neurologist, and except for one odd trait we got along well. That one trait was that Dave was *cheap*—not with his family, his friends, or me— but with his secretaries.

In those days, with the exception of patient care, medical secretaries took care of everything in the office. They answered phones and scheduled appointments; they greeted new patients and had them fill out forms; they inventoried and ordered all office supplies; they typed the consultation reports and follow-up notes dictated by the doctors; they took the doctors' white coats to the laundry and brought them back again; they did all the filing, billing, and collections; and in between patients, they ran back to the exam rooms and changed the sheets and pillowcases on the exam tables. A good medical secretary was superhuman.

Dave and I each had our own secretary, and mine was a jewel. Joanne Ferdina was a former model who laughed at my jokes and performed the full complement of secretarial tasks flawlessly—all with a cigarette dangling from her lower lip.

Dave's secretaries, on the other hand, were young and new to the business, compensating for their lack of experience with intelligence and hard work. But for some reason, after three or four months they would all quit.

Although having to replace a steady stream of secretaries seemed terribly inconvenient, Dave was just fine with it. As soon as his current secretary had given him her two-week notice, Dave would call the employment agency, interview a few prospects, and hire another young, inexperienced secretary to take her place.

Although I thought this was a little strange, I said nothing about it. Then one evening after our secretaries had left for the day, Dave explained the reasoning behind his secretarial turnover.

In those days the convention was that new secretaries were hired on a provisional basis at low starting salaries, and if they worked out, a few weeks later they received raises, followed by periodic raises after that. After six months they got health insurance, and after a year they qualified for the office retirement plan.

But Dave's secretaries followed a different trajectory. Dave invariably hired bright, inexperienced women at low starting salaries. To prove themselves they worked hard, and when they had learned the job, they expected a performance review and a raise. But when weeks passed and performance reviews and raises were never mentioned, they assumed that Dr. Rich was still not satisfied with their work, and they worked even harder: bringing plants to the office, having Dave's morning coffee ready when he arrived, straightening his desk, and spending extra time collecting his patient's bad debts. But no matter how diligently or creatively they worked, the performance reviews and raises never came, and eventually they resigned in frustration.

As Dave was happily describing his method, I pictured Pavlov's rats pressing the bars in their boxes faster and faster in the hope of being rewarded with food pellets. But in the case of Dave's secretaries, the pellets never came. Although this saved Dave some money, it seemed like a pretty sleazy way to treat another person.

Around this same time Don Dixon, president of the Adventist Medical Center, called me to set up a lunch meeting at a restaurant not far from the new medical center complex. The meeting, he said, was to discuss the possibility of my becoming Adventist's full-time neurologist.

But before telling you about the meeting, first you need a little background information. Since I am now old, I, like most people my age, spend a lot of time remembering the past, and not infrequently one of the many awful things I've done will pop into my head. When this happens, I'll close my eyes, grit my teeth, and mutter, "Oh, God, now why did I do that?" My meeting with Don Dixon at the Acapulco Restaurant is such a memory.

Your next piece of background information has to do with smoking. It was 1977, and although the surgeon general had been stamping warnings on cigarette packs since 1965, most doctors who smoked blithely continued doing so, myself included.

I'll place the blame for that on one of my role models—my father— who was both a very good surgeon and a very good smoker. As a child I often tagged along while my father made his Sunday rounds, where his routine went something like this: he would arrive on the surgical ward puffing on a fresh El Producto Bouquet cigar, the charge nurse would gather up his patients' charts, a nursing student would grab an ashtray, and off we'd go. At the door to each of his patient's rooms, my father would lay his cigar in the ashtray; the poor nursing student remaining in the hall while the rest of us entered the room. Obviously, things have changed since then.

Finally, you should know that ideally Adventists do not drink beverages containing caffeine or alcohol, nor do they smoke, eat meat, or use pepper. But as with any religion, many Adventists don't follow these practices, though responsible Adventists in public positions—such as hospital administrators—usually do.

On the day of our meeting, Don Dixon and a couple of his junior executives met me at the Acapulco Restaurant. At that time, I was six feet, two inches tall and weighed somewhere between 250 and 260 pounds, while none of the hospital administrators weighed more than 140 lbs. When the maître d' seated us in a booth, I sat on one side of the table and the three administrators sat on the other.

The waitress came by and asked if we would like something to drink before lunch. The Adventists said no; I ordered a beer. Then after drinking my beer, I felt the need for a cigarette and asked if they would mind if I smoked. When they said no, I whipped out my Marlboros and fired up.

My boorish behavior must have made the poor Adventists regret the offer they were about to make me, but to their credit and my good fortune, they just kept smiling and stayed on message. Don Dixon described the future that he envisioned for the new hospital and how I would help make that happen, and then he offered me a job.

A couple of weeks later, I called Don to accept his offer, told Dave Rich that I was leaving, and moved all my books and office furniture into Suite 205 of the newly completed professional office building—future home of the East Portland Neurology Clinic.

At the new Adventist Medical Center, I met both the older physicians who had staffed the hospital for years and the younger physicians, many of whom, like me, were hoping to make a go of it in the newly expanded medical environment. Collectively it was a wonderful group, and I liked them all; in return, they kept me very busy.

One of the young doctors at Adventist was a family practitioner by the name of Tom Hoggard. He, like many of the primary care doctors, would call me from time to time to discuss his patients with neurologic problems. Tom was a friendly, likeable guy, and one day after we had finished talking medicine, he asked if I was married. I confessed that I was divorced, and when Tom said that he was too, I suggested that we get together for a beer—but then we made no plans. But a few days later when we talked again, Tom asked me if I played tennis, which was then the hot recreational activity for young adults, and when I said that I did, we set a time to meet at one of the city's public courts.

Walking back to our cars after tennis, Tom mentioned that he played the guitar. I have no memory of why he said that, but I replied that once upon a time I had played the drums. Then Tom suggested that we meet again, this time with our instruments in the basement of his house.

It was an exciting and confusing moment. Until then I had completely forgotten about how much I once loved drumming. How, I wondered, could I have done that? I must have thought that unless you were a professional musician, playing in a band was something that you just did as a kid. But could I play in a band again at the age of thirty-six? Well, maybe. After all, here was this seemingly sane, presumably responsible physician suggesting that we get together to play some music, and it had sounded very attractive. So I said yes.

But first I would need another set of drums. Because I was pursuing a grown-up career in medicine, I had assumed that I would never need them again and had foolishly sold my old Slingerland drums. But fortunately I had had the good sense to save all those beautiful Zildjian cymbals, which were packed away somewhere back at my house.

But where would I find another set of drums? Driving around town I had seen a store on Southeast Hawthorne Boulevard with pictures of instruments and sound equipment painted on its walls and windows, and that seemed as good a place as any to look for a used set of drums. The next day I walked into Showcase Music and Sound, where I met John Chassaing, one of the store's owners, and told him that I was looking for a used drum kit. John pointed to a set of black and white drums stacked on a shelf above the counter.

Although they looked very cool, except for their rims and heads, the drums were made of plastic. My old drums had been made of maple, which was then the industry standard. When I mentioned this to John, he said that because of their plastic shells they were known among drummers as "Jelly Beans," and even though they were made of plastic, they sounded great. And that was enough for me.

Tom and I played together several times, and though it felt good to be playing music again, it quickly became obvious that if we wanted to sound like a real band, we would need a few more instruments, as well as a singer—especially a singer. Tom had been both singing and playing the guitar, and though he was a good guitar player, he wasn't much of a vocalist.

But then Tom said that an architect friend of his by the name of Alan Beard had recently broken up with a dental hygienist he'd been dating. Her name was Patti Dunahugh, and although Tom had never heard her sing, she was supposed to be a real singer—and a good one. Tom asked if he should ask her to join us some night, and I said yes. A few days later, Tom called to say that Patti would be at our next practice.

The first night that Patti Dunahugh played with us, she blew into Tom's basement like a whirlwind, a guitar case in one hand and a satchel full of sheet music in the other. She was very attractive—a tall, slim brunette—but all business. I was sitting behind my drums when she arrived. Tom tossed out a quick "Patti, this is Bob," and Patti shot me a "Hi, Bob," on her way to the music stand at the front of the room, where she unpacked the music and strapped on her guitar. "So," she said, "what should we play?"

Tom gave her the titles of a couple of the things we'd been working on, Patti found the music, and we began playing. It was a little rough at first, but Patti took control, telling us what to play and when to play it. Though this caused Tom and I to exchange a few questioning glances, the music was so much better than what we had been making on our own that we kept our mouths shut and allowed her to direct us.

23

After a couple of hours Patti gathered up her music, returned her guitar to its case, and said, "Sorry guys, but I've got to go. Same time next week?"

We mumbled something in the affirmative and thanked her for coming, and she was gone.

The three of us played together a few more weeks. Then one afternoon Tom called to say that Bart McMullen, one of Adventist Medical Center's internists, played the saxophone.

"Should I invite him to play with us?" Tom asked.

"Sure," I said. "Invite Bart, too."

The Invitation

The annual Adventist Medical Center banquet was always in January, and at its 1979 gathering Tom and I were seated at different tables. Although I attached no particular significance to this, Tom was sitting where he was because Bart McMullan was at the same table.

While waiting for their food to arrive, Tom leaned over to Bart and said, "I hear you play the saxophone."

Surprised, Bart replied, "You're right, Tom, but it's more like I played the saxophone. It's been a while, at least twenty years." But then, recalling his saxophone-playing days more precisely (Bart was a pretty precise guy), he cleared his throat and corrected himself.

"I'm sorry, Tom, but what I said wasn't right. I just remembered that I took my saxophone with me to submarine school—so that would make it eleven years instead of twenty. But either way, it's been a while since I played."

Then Tom smiled and asked, "You still have your saxophone, don't you?"

"Yes, Tom," Bart said, now smiling, too. "I still have it. Why do you ask?"

Tom leaned closer.

"Because a few of us have started playing at my house on Wednesday nights. Bob Crumpacker plays the drums, I play the guitar, and a girl named Patti sings. We'd love to have you join us. Drop by some Wednesday and see what you think."

"I appreciate the invitation, Tom," Bart said, "but I'll need to think about it."

A couple of weeks later, Tom saw Bart at the hospital and asked if he'd thought any more about joining us. This time, Bart said that he would come.

CHAPTER 3: TOM

Tom Hoggard was an easy man to be around. Although he was big—a shade under six feet, broad shouldered, and sturdily built—he never seemed imposing. When he talked his eyes looked squarely into yours, and his smile was welcoming. His speech was slow and warm, like syrup over pancakes, and if you listened closely, you'd hear the faintest hint of a Southern drawl. Invariably polite and always attentive, he smiled often and laughed easily, and if he was ever angry I never saw it.

By the time he'd asked Bart to play with us, Tom and I had shared some patients, a few games of tennis, and several nights of music, enough for me to realize that Tom had a talent for working with people. But I should stress that there was nothing self-serving about Tom's interest in people. Although I can't say that he was entirely altruistic in his dealings with others, his intent was never more than to share in whatever benefits their association produced.

The fact was that Tom needed people. They were absolutely essential to his well-being. He was curious about them, found them endlessly fascinating, and was at his absolute best when he was around them—the more the merrier.

Not surprisingly, Tom's interest in people and the care that he showed them had earned him a large network of friends and acquaintances, and because of his curiosity, he knew their histories, their likes and dislikes, and any special talents they might have.

Although Tom enjoyed hosting large events—picnics, parties, meetings, and entertainments of various kinds—he took particular pleasure in putting together smaller groups for some special purpose that would benefit everyone, himself included. In other words, exactly what he was doing with the band.

27

THE LOVEHANDLES

Tom Hoggard's story really begins with his grandfather whose long, colorful, and productive life included two periods of military service and simultaneous careers in medicine, education, banking, and business.

At the age of twenty-one, John Thomas Hoggard left his home in Aulander, North Carolina, to fight with Teddy Roosevelt's Rough Riders in the Spanish-American War. Returning home, he earned degrees from the University of North Carolina and the Medical College of Virginia. After serving in World War I as a military surgeon, he began a long and respected career as a general practitioner, a profession that in those days included performing surgery and delivering babies, often in difficult circumstances.

Tom tells the story of one stormy night when a young man knocked on his grandfather's door to tell him that his wife was in labor and needed him immediately. The Hoggards were then living in Atkinson, North Carolina, while the young couple lived several miles away on the other side of the Black River.

Dr. Hoggard and his wife dressed quickly, hooked up their horse-drawn buggy, and drove to the Black River, which was crossed on a small ferry that was pulled across the river by rope. During the crossing, their horse was startled by a flash of lightning and dove into the river, pulling the carriage in along with it. But the Hoggards remained on board, crossed the river, walked to the couple's home, and successfully delivered their baby.

Dr. Hoggard's career in education began in 1935 when he was elected chairman of the New Hanover County Board of Education, a position that he held until 1952. He was also instrumental in founding Wilmington College and served as its president from 1952 until 1958 and as its chairman of the board from 1952 until his death in 1965. Under his leadership, Wilmington College grew from a two-year junior college to a four-year state college, and eventually became the University of North Carolina Wilmington.

Because of his many contributions to education, Wilmington's John T. Hoggard High School and the University of North Carolina Wilmington's John T. Hoggard Hall were named in his honor.

In banking, Dr. Hoggard helped organize the Morris Plan Bank of Wilmington, which then became the Bank of Wilmington, and served as its vice president for many years. He was also chairman of the board for the North Carolina National Bank, which later became the Bank of America.

He was an active member of innumerable boards, clubs, societies, and charitable organizations, as well as the founder and president of the New Hanover Housing Corporation and Tom's Drug Company, a pharmacy that is still in operation today.

Pictures of Dr. Hoggard show a large, powerfully built man whose dark eyes and strong features gave him a stern, uncompromising appearance. When I asked Tom to describe his grandfather, his initial response was to say that he was "scary," explaining that although his grandfather was a charming man who loved to tell jokes and pull pranks, there was also something forbidding about him, as though earning his displeasure should be avoided at all costs.

His grandchildren called him "Papa," but none of the other family members—including his wife—called him anything but "Dr. Hoggard."

Despite Tom's feeling that angering his grandfather could be dangerous, the doctor's firstborn son, John Thomas Hoggard, Jr., had a rebellious streak that frequently put him at odds with his father. Although John Thomas could have worked for any of his father's many enterprises, he was determined to be his own man, and became an accountant and independent businessman. Together with his sister and younger brother, John Thomas founded the Hoggard Company, which operated a wholesale dry goods business and a vending machine company.

When the United States entered World War II, instead of using his family connections to become an officer, John Thomas enlisted in the Navy. While his ship was undergoing repairs in Bremerton, Washington, John Thomas hitchhiked to Portland, where he met a beautiful young woman by the name of Lenore Elkins. The attraction was mutual, and their chance meeting was followed by a chaotic courtship of calls and visits whenever and wherever John Thomas was in port. They married during a layover in Los Angeles.

Lenore was soon pregnant, but rather than move to North Carolina and be among strangers, she stayed in Oregon with her family, and on March 13, 1944, John Thomas Hoggard III—our own Tom Hoggard—was born.

After the war, John Thomas spent four years with his wife's family in Oregon, where a second son, Robert, and a third son, Edmund, were born. Then the Hoggards moved to North Carolina, where John Thomas resumed his work as an accountant and businessman.

But just when his future must have seemed the brightest, John Thomas had the first attack of a mysterious neurologic ailment that was eventually diagnosed as multiple sclerosis. More attacks followed, and though each was followed by a transient period of improvement, his overall course was downhill.

John Thomas saw the best specialists in North Carolina, but they all told him the same thing: that multiple sclerosis was untreatable. So with nothing to lose he decided to seek help elsewhere, and the first place that he looked was faith healing. But after being "healed" by famed evangelist Oral Roberts, John Thomas was no better, and continued his search for something that would make a difference.

On his next try, he got lucky—or so he thought. John Thomas consulted a chiropractor who told him that chiropractic medicine could cure his multiple sclerosis. Convinced that his prayers had been answered, John Thomas went all in. But after months of treatment, he failed to improve, and was told that his only hope was an intensive course of treatment at the Spears Chiropractic Hospital in Denver. Now desperate, John Thomas agreed to go, but following a protracted stay at the chiropractic hospital he returned to North Caroline unchanged.

When Tom was fifteen, his father made one final attempt to return to productivity and leased a restaurant in Wrightsville Beach, an exclusive coastal community ten miles east of Wilmington. But beset by a number of problems, not least of which was his own failing health, the restaurant closed after one summer of operation. John Thomas would never work again.

Then, as if John Thomas's problems were not enough, Lenore was diagnosed with a brain tumor and referred to the Johns Hopkins Hospital in Baltimore for treatment. With both parents incapacitated, it was decided that Tom, who had just turned sixteen and recently earned his driver's license, should drive his mother to Baltimore and then continue on to Oregon, where the boys would live with their grandparents until their parents could join them.

Tom was now the responsible adult, and with the family's 1953 Mercury station wagon loaded down with Tom, his mother and brothers, their suitcases, their cherished possessions, and the family dog, Tom drove north to Baltimore, said goodbye to his mother, then turned west toward Oregon. But three hundred miles later, the car broke down at a truck stop in North Lima, Ohio, and Tom was told that it would need a new engine.

Since a new engine would cost nearly everything that he'd been given for the trip, Tom wanted to discuss this with his mother first, but when he tried to reach her, she had just had surgery and was unable to talk. The best he could do was leave her a message explaining their predicament and ask that she call him when she could.

Tom paid for the engine, which would arrive from out of state in several days. In the meantime, the boys had to eat and sleep, and though they could sleep in the car, there wasn't much money left for food. But when news of their plight spread throughout the truck stop, the truckers generously stepped forward to pay for their meals.

Then when Lenore was well enough to address the boys' situation, she called the Ohio Highway Patrol and asked them to find her sons. When the boys had been located she told Tom that money would be wired to a local bank, and when the car was ready he should them drive back to North Carolina. Their next trip to Oregon, would be by train.

In Wilmington, the boys bought three tickets to Oregon, a journey that would take nearly a week. Although the trip would require several train changes, the only change they would make after sundown would come the first night.

That night, the boys arrived at the station and waited inside for their next train. But when the train's arrival was announced, Tom couldn't find the tickets. The boys searched every piece of clothing and luggage in their possession, but the tickets weren't there. The only place left to look was in the train car that they had just left.

Locating the stationmaster, Tom explained their situation and found a sympathetic ear. The stationmaster agreed to hold the train while they looked for their tickets, even giving them a flashlight to help with their search.

But rushing out onto the station platform the boys discovered that their car had been uncoupled from the rest of the train and moved to another set of tracks—but no one seemed to know which tracks those were. Following the flashlight's beam, they searched the entire yard, climbing over couplings and stumbling over tracks until they found their car and the missing tickets. Returning to the station, they thanked the stationmaster and boarded the next train. It had been the most frightening night of Tom's life.

In Oregon, the boys were met by their grandparents and driven to the farm. In the past, visiting the farm had always been a treat. Although there were animals to be fed, eggs to be gathered, and cows to be milked, the boys loved the work, and they would quickly adapt to their new home.

But school was another matter. In Wilmington, their classmates were often the sons and daughters of elite members of Wilmington society, but in Oregon, the students were more often the offspring of farmers and loggers: men who lived hard, drank hard, and settled their differences with their fists. In North Carolina, the Hoggard name had assured them of preferential treatment, but in Oregon, they were outsiders whose status was yet to be determined.

Tom missed his old life acutely, but knew that it was gone forever. His father was dying, his mother's fate unknown, and for the first time in his life, Tom was depressed. In addition, the sadness that he felt was worsened by inactivity and improved by physical activity—the harder, the better. And though Tom had been an excellent student in North Carolina, he now abandoned his studies in favor of farm work and sports.

One day a classmate challenged Tom to a fight. Although Tom had done some boxing in North Carolina, what took place in Oregon was no gentleman's boxing match. The boy charged Tom, wrestled him to the ground, and flailed at him with both fists, breaking his nose. Tom fought back and managed to blacken one of the boy's eyes, ending the fight in a draw.

When Tom got home, his grandfather saw his face and asked him what had happened. After listening to Tom's story, the old man went to the attic and brought down two pairs of boxing gloves. He would teach Tom how to fight "Oregon style," and as they put on the gloves, his grandfather began talking.

"Never fight unless you have to," he said. "Avoid it if you can, but if you have to fight, you fight to win."

Then shadow boxing to illustrate his words, his grandfather explained what Tom should do in various situations and concluded the lesson by saying, "Once you get a reputation as someone who'll stand up for himself, you'll never be bothered again."

It wasn't long before his grandfather's words were tested. One evening as Tom was walking to a school dance, he passed a group of young men standing near the gymnasium door. When one of them called his name, Tom turned in time to see the man swinging for his head. But Tom ducked under the blow and came up fast, catching him on the jaw with a solid right. The man went down, unconscious, and just as his grandfather had said, Tom was never bothered again.

Several months after the boys arrived in Oregon, their parents joined them. Although their father wasn't doing well and went to a nursing home, their mother's brain tumor had responded to treatment, and she rented a small house for the four of them in the nearby town of Molalla. Although this gave the boys some measure of stability, Tom remained depressed.

THE LOVEHANDLES

When Tom's senior year arrived, his grades were barely good enough to keep him eligible for sports. Recognizing his struggle and hoping to provide some structure to Tom's life, his high school football coach—and the commanding officer of the local Army National Guard—convinced Tom to join the Guard.

Tom found the routine of military training helpful, but once again his world was about to be torn apart. Tom had been dating a classmate by the name of Jackie, and when Jackie told him that she was pregnant Tom was stunned. The idea of being married and a father at eighteen was overwhelming, but Tom gathered his courage and proposed.

Then as the end of his senior year approached, Tom was found to be half a credit short of being able to graduate. He pleaded with the school administrators, but they couldn't help him. Instead, they referred him to the school's vocational counselor, who took one look at Tom's sorry academic record and suggested that he consider a career in logging.

That summer, Tom served six months of active duty at Fort Ord in California, and though he and Jackie returned to Oregon with a beautiful daughter, he had no plans for the future. Unable to afford a house or apartment, Tom and his new family moved into his mother's garage.

Then Tom found a job clearing brush from electrical power lines and burning it, but when the job ended, his employer refused to pay him. Then his father died, and though this came as no surprise, it was one more loss to absorb, and at that point, Tom felt hopeless.

But one morning Tom's grandmother, a former teacher and school principal, told him to get in the car, and without saying where they were going, drove him to the GED testing center.

"Go take the test," she said, "You'll pass."

He passed.

Then his grandmother told him that he would be attending Mount Angel College, a small four-year school only fifteen miles from Molalla, and with the prospect of a college education, Tom's future seemed a little brighter.

During his first year at Mount Angel, Tom's depression began to lift, and for the first time in years he was able to study. After two years at Mount Angel, his grades were good enough to transfer to the Oregon College of Education (OCE) in Monmouth, a much larger school that was still only forty-eight miles from Molalla.

Although Tom had considered becoming a doctor, many of the people on his mother's side of the family were teachers, and at first Tom thought that he, too, might become a teacher. But midway through his time at OCE, Tom knew that he wanted to be a doctor, and switched to a pre-med curriculum.

During the summers, Tom worked at a sawmill, and after graduation he took a job with the Polk County Health and Sanitation Department inspecting restaurants and migrant farm camps. Then two years after their daughter Debbie's birth, Tom and Jackie had a second daughter, Diane.

Despite his busy life, Tom graduated from OCE with excellent grades and applied to medical school. Although his academic record was less than perfect, the University of Oregon Medical School staff was intrigued with his life story, and Tom became the first graduate from OCE to be admitted to medical school.

Medical school passed quickly and Tom interned at Gorgas Army Hospital in Panama. At Gorgas he was not only given the freedom to practice everything he had learned in medical school but he was also introduced to the fascinating world of tropical diseases, a branch of medicine practically unknown to American doctors.

At Gorgas, Tom tried to find a specialty that he liked, but when every field seemed equally interesting, he decided to become a family practitioner. He applied to OHSU and was accepted to their family practice program.

At OHSU, one of Tom's clinical instructors was Dr. "Red" Irvine, who along with his brother, Harry, and Avelo "Av" Caldwell, staffed the Mount Tabor Family Practice Clinic in Portland. Tom developed a deep respect for Red, who had been both a vice president of the American Academy of Family Practice and a chairman of the American Board of Family Medicine. Tom worked hard for Red; in turn Red was impressed with Tom. And when Red mentioned that his group was looking for a new associate, Tom was interested.

Although he knew that it would have been better to finish his residency, by then Tom had a wife, two daughters, and a considerable amount of student debt, and was anxious to begin making a living. So, after the second year of his residency, Tom left OHSU to join the Mount Tabor Family Practice Clinic.

Through all of Tom's ups and downs, music was in his life. His mother and grandmother both played the piano, and his uncle played several instruments and was the leader of a local dance orchestra.

In junior high, Tom had asked his parents for a Gene Autry guitar, and after mastering a few chords, he'd entered a school talent show. With a friend playing piano and Tom singing and playing the guitar, they had performed a couple of Ricky Nelson songs. Tom still smiles when he remembers the girls screaming.

After moving to Oregon, Tom bought an electric guitar and joined a country western band called the Travelers, but because he was underage, whenever the band played bars Tom would have to go outside during breaks.

At OCE, Tom was a member of a band called Justus 4, a group that wore matching smoking jackets with shiny lapels. Although Tom was too busy to join a band in medical school, he kept a set of drums and an electric guitar in his basement so that during parties he and his friends could get together and jam.

CHAPTER 4: HOUSES

Since moving to Portland in 1974, by 1979 I had lived in a number of houses—five to be exact. After arriving in town, I rented a house in Parkrose, a subdivision of ranch-style homes on the eastern edge of the city. I lived there for eight or ten months, then bought a house in Lake Oswego, a suburb eight miles south of Portland. Although my home in Lake Oswego was on the lake and even had its own motorboat, after a few months I sold it and rented a tiny Craftsman house in southeast Portland not far from my office. But after a few months I again grew restless and bought another home on Mount Tabor, an inactive volcano on the east side of town.

Mount Tabor gave Portland the distinction of being one of only four U.S. cities with a volcano within its city limits. My home on Mount Tabor had an unobstructed view of still another volcano—this time an active one—the perfectly conical, ten-thousand-foot-high Mount Saint Helens in Washington State.

My Mount Tabor home was essentially a one-level ranch-style home with a separate apartment in its daylight basement. It was more house than I needed, but my sister, Nancy, and her boyfriend, Rick, had both graduated from medical school in 1976 and moved to Portland to do their residencies at OHSU—Nancy's in internal medicine and oncology, and Rick's in internal medicine. Because the main floor of my Mount Tabor house was big enough for me, I asked Nancy and Rick if they would like to rent the basement apartment—and they did.

Rick wasn't just an excellent internist, he also had a keen interest in marijuana, and one day he asked me if he could grow a few plants in one of the basement's unused rooms. I said sure, why not, and promptly forgot about it.

THE LOVEHANDLES

Then one day I had to call a plumber. The plumber that I got was an older gentleman of the kindly grandfather variety, who assessed the problem and said that he could fix it, but he first needed to turn off the water. Since I had no idea where the water valve was, the plumber and I began looking through the basement rooms. The valve, of course, was in Rick's plant room, and when I opened the door we were confronted by a small forest of young, healthy marijuana plants clustered beneath the grow lights hanging from the ceiling. Unfortunately, this was in pre-legalization days when anything to do with marijuana—even in ultra-liberal Portland—was accompanied by a generous measure of paranoia, and my first reaction was to hope that the plumber wouldn't report me.

But the plumber's reaction was surprisingly mild. He began by saying, "Well, you certainly have . . ." and paused a moment before adding, ". . . a green thumb, don't you?" Then he picked his way through Rick's plants and turned off the water. Nothing more was said about the marijuana. He did his job, I paid him, and he left.

Although the plumber had given no indication that he was alarmed by what he had seen, as a doctor I couldn't take a chance, and when Rick came home that night I told him what had happened and asked him to destroy the plants. He did so without complaint.

Now if you've been counting the houses that I've lived in so far, you know that I still have one to go. And sure enough, after occupying the Mount Tabor house for a few months, I again grew restless and began thinking about my next home.

Except for the Lake Oswego house, all my other homes had been in southeast Portland, and this time I was thinking about something west of the Willamette River, in either the southwest or northwest quadrants of the city. With this in mind, I found a realtor familiar with that part of the city and we began looking at houses.

What the . . .?

At about that time, I began to suspect that my desire for still another home was the result of some deep-seated psychological disorder, perhaps some kind of exotic compulsion. And even as I continued looking at homes, my conscious mind was wondering what in the world was wrong with me. But whatever it was, it was out of my control.

With this strange push-pull going on in my head, I found some flaw in every home I looked that prevented me from buying it. The realtor, however, was on to me, and after a few unsuccessful house-hunting trips, she began asking me exactly what I did or didn't like about the home I had just rejected. She continued doing this until I had given her a comprehensive list of all the qualities that I was and wasn't looking for in my ideal home.

Although I would have preferred looking at homes indefinitely, she found a house that fit all the apparent criteria of my ideal home. Although I wanted to tell her no, no, no, just keep showing me houses, I had run out of excuses. So I bought the house.

Now the owner of a beautiful home in Portland's West Hills, I had such a severe case of buyer's remorse that had there been a homeowner's ICU, I would have been there on life support.

So, you may be asking, what was this peculiar compulsion of mine all about? I now believe it was the result of two real needs, but only one of them had anything to do with houses.

Since moving to Oregon, I had made one important discovery about myself, which was that wherever I lived I had to see the sky, and the more sky I saw the better. I'm certain that this came from growing up in Kansas, where 180 degrees of sky were always visible.

But this wasn't Kansas. Though sometimes flat, Oregon was more often hilly, occasionally mountainous, and frequently covered with tall trees and dense vegetation. Add to that Oregon's well-known tendency for overcast and rainy days, and you have a very un-Kansas-like environment.

THE LOVEHANDLES

I made this discovery about myself while living in Lake Oswego. Although most of the world's population would have committed any number of crimes against man and nature to live in a lakeside house with its own motorboat, the homes surrounding Oswego Lake were themselves surrounded by hills covered with big trees and thick greenery, and it felt like I was living at the bottom of a deep, dark hole.

But my Lake Oswego home was the only residence that I had a legitimate reason for leaving. My other moves had nothing to do with the houses. Instead, they had to do with love. I'll explain.

By then it was 1979, and I was thirty-eight years old and single, my only marriage having been during my senior year of medical school. But the marriage had become moribund quickly, and was essentially over two years later. On paper my marriage looked great, but the *feeling* just wasn't there, and there was nothing I could do about that. The fault was mine: my proposal hasty and unwise, and I took full responsibility for the error. But having been part of an unsuccessful marriage didn't mean that I had lost faith in either love or marriage—not at all.

In college I had been in a three-year relationship with a girl that I was crazy about, but through my own stupidity and insecurity, I'd lost her. And though that relationship ended badly, the feeling of loving someone and being loved in return had been so wonderful that I longed to experience it again. The catch was that the loss I had suffered was so painful I couldn't risk going through it again. I was caught in between two strong, conflicting emotions, and as a result I ended up in a series of safe, loveless relationships that were pleasant but ultimately doomed to fail.

The process of looking for houses was in some way tied to my search for love. Although it sounds a little weird, I'm certain that it's true. I thought that finding the right house would somehow lead me to the right woman. Why? I have no idea.

The problem with my newest home was that although it had an open view of the sky, it had been designed for a family, not some lovelorn bachelor. It was a three-story, thirty-five-hundred-square-foot house with four bedrooms and high ceilings, but its spaciousness made me feel more alone than I had felt in all my previous homes combined.

In addition, my new house had a number of wonderful design features—hardwood floors, leaded windows, mahogany woodwork, and monk doors—that screamed for the right furniture, lighting, and art to bring them to life, but I had neither the talent nor the interest to attempt that on my own. In my limited worldview, decorating a home was something that your wife did.

Adding to my sense of isolation, I ended up living out of just four of the home's twelve rooms: one bedroom, one bathroom, the kitchen, and every so often, the laundry room in the basement. The other rooms sat empty, accumulating dust, and instead of making me happy, my new home only added to my misery.

A *House Beautiful* description from those days might have read, "The doctor's principal living area is the master bedroom, where a collection of striking yellow drapes in a bold floral pattern hang in excess over the windows, saying a firm 'no' to natural light. These majestic tapestries once adorned the living room of the doctor's childhood home but here exceed their windows' length by several feet, settling into impressive piles on the floor below.

"The bedroom itself is cohesively furnished with an unmade king-sized bed, tastefully covered with a cheap red bedspread certain to fail even the most casual black light encounter. In addition, an antiquated twenty-one-inch TV playfully sporting a pair of tinfoiled rabbit ear antennae sits within easy reach at the bedside. It is a home that any lonely, middle-aged physician would be proud to call his own."

CHAPTER 5: LARRY FRANKS

My saving graces in those days were my work, my friends, and the band. Fortunately, I was so busy at work that I had little time to dwell on either my newest house or my marital situation. Instead, I would work late, grab some fast food, drive home, and fall asleep in front of the TV.

One morning in 1975, I was in the Portland Adventist ICU examining a patient who had suffered a brain hemorrhage the night before—most likely from a ruptured cerebral aneurysm—and whose life was hanging by a thread.

In addition to the aorta, as in Patti Dunahugh's case, aneurysms can arise from one or more of several arteries in the head due to congenital (meaning present at birth) areas of weakness in their walls. Over the course of a person's life, these weak spots may enlarge until they burst.

When a brain aneurysm ruptures, it's usually bad news. Forty percent of the time it will result in death; if the patient survives, then 65 percent of the time it will leave them with a significant brain injury. Like I said, it's not a good thing.

As I was standing in Portland Adventist Hospital's ICU examining this patient, Adventist's president, Don Dixon, accompanied by a couple of his junior administrators, entered the ICU behind a very large young man. Don looked around the room and spotted me, bringing the large young man with him to my patient's bedside. The young man's name was Larry Franks. He had just completed his neurosurgery residency and was now touring the country looking at various practice opportunities.

Larry Franks was a couple of inches taller than me, and had the thick neck and athletic frame more often seen on tight ends than neurosurgeons. Shaking his hand was like putting on a catcher's mitt.

Looking down at the patient, Larry Franks said, "What you got here, doc?"

"Ruptured aneurysm," I said. "Came in last night. The neurosurgeon wants my opinion regarding surgery."

Franks reached down and opened the man's eyelids. Both pupils were fully dilated and failed to constrict upon exposure to light, two ominous findings known in the trade as "fixed and dilated."

"Doesn't look good," Franks said.

"No," I said, "he's going to cool."

Although Dr. Franks had given no indication that what I had just said—"he's going to cool"—had just sold him on both me and Portland Adventist Hospital, in the years to come I would repeatedly hear Larry say that those words were the reason why he came to Portland—an honor that I'll always treasure.

A couple of months after our ICU encounter, Larry Franks called me to say that he had decided to practice at Adventist. He said he would be arriving in Portland later that day to rent an apartment, and was I free to have dinner with him that night? I said I was.

We ate at a restaurant on the corner of Northeast 122nd Avenue and Halsey Street called The Refectory (which is still there, the last time I checked), and after that we picked up a couple of six-packs and went to his new apartment to drink and quiz each other on obscure neurology and neurosurgery facts and trivia.

By nature doctors are very competitive, and our neurological information game gave me a chance to see just how phenomenally smart—and funny—this Larry Franks really was. Then after we had consumed all the beer, we decided that we needed more beer. But as we were preparing to leave his apartment, Larry discovered that he was out of cash, and when I checked my wallet, I found that I was, too. But then I remembered that there was an ATM just up the street.

"Not a problem, doctor," I told him confidently. "We can hit an ATM on our way to the 7-Eleven."

Larry cocked his head like a dog hearing an unfamiliar sound.

"An ATM?" he asked. "What's an ATM?"

Larry had never heard of an ATM. This was not due to any deficiency on his part but because he had done his surgical training in Canada, where the banks were not yet equipped with ATMs.

I tried to explain an ATM to him: how you drove to a bank that had one, put a plastic card into a slot, and entered your password. Then you indicated how much money you wanted, and providing that you had performed every step of the process flawlessly and your account had sufficient funds, the ATM would give you the money.

But after repeated explanations, Larry was still having trouble with the concept. Either he was too drunk to understand or I was too drunk to give him a reasonable explanation—or both—but he kept saying things like, "You can't be serious. There's a machine that will give you money?" and "Doctor, are you sure there's not someone hiding inside the ATM?"

Although I answered his questions to the best of my ability, Larry was still not convinced that such a thing as an ATM really existed. Finally, I decided that the only way to convince him was by taking him to an actual ATM, which I did, and to Larry's delight and amazement, it gave us enough money to buy more beer. It was one of the funniest nights of my life.

To do their best work, neurologists need access to good neurosurgeons, and vice versa. It's a symbiotic relationship. Although I had had the good fortune of working alongside several exceptional neurosurgeons, Larry was by far the best neurosurgeon I ever worked with. Technically, there was no area of neurosurgery that he didn't excel in; those oversized mitts could do anything and make it look easy.

Several years before, during my internship at Good Samaritan Hospital, I had worked with one of the Northwest's most revered neurosurgeons. This man had gained a reputation for his uncanny skill in operating on cerebral aneurysms among other things, and as a result, doctors from all over the state would send their patients to Good Samaritan for him to operate.

But in reality, as good as he was in other areas, his record with aneurysms was abysmal. In the two months that I was on his service

THE LOVEHANDLES

I had watched him perform at least half a dozen aneurysm surgeries, and every one of the patients died. Aneurysms, I concluded, were just difficult to operate.

But one of the first cases that I asked Larry to see was a young woman with—you guessed it—a ruptured cerebral aneurysm. I know, I know. You probably think that all doctors in Portland do is take care of people with aneurysms, but I can assure you that's not the case. We see the same cross-section of problems that doctors in any large city see. It's just that so far, I've had no reason to talk about those other problems. But be patient, and I will.

Anyway, the lady with the ruptured aneurysm was very sick; so sick, in fact, that my expectations for any surgery that Larry might perform weren't great. But Larry was ecstatic. He said that he loved to operate on aneurysms and it would be his first aneurysm since coming to Portland, and thank you, doctor, thank you for asking him to see her. But despite his enthusiasm, I wasn't convinced that Larry could do any better than the neurosurgeon at Good Samaritan.

Although there are several ways of operating on an aneurysm, the one used most often is called "clipping" the aneurysm. This is done by placing a little V-shaped metal clip across the base of the aneurysm and squeezing it shut, cutting off the aneurysm's blood supply so that it can't rupture again. And that was exactly what Larry did for the woman that I had sent him.

Following the surgery, Larry called me to thank me again for the referral. The case, he said, had gone well, and he thought she would recover nicely. "That's terrific," I answered, but I wasn't convinced. Both my experience with aneurysm surgeries generally and my lack of experience with Larry's aneurysm surgeries specifically warned me not to expect too much. Besides that, the thought of Larry's big paws dissecting out a fragile aneurysm and placing a tiny clip across its base didn't add to my confidence.

The next morning, I decided to stop by the ICU to see how the woman was really doing, and after putting on the required gown, gloves, and mask, I walked into her room to find her awake and sitting in a chair beside the bed, talking to her family. Although I tried not to look surprised, I probably failed miserably.

Of course, not all aneurysm cases can or should be operated. Many patients are in such dire straits after their initial bleed—like the patient I was seeing when Larry and I first met—that surgery makes no sense. At best, aneurysm surgery only prevents the aneurysm from bleeding again; it can't fix a badly damaged brain. But for those patients who were healthy enough to be operated, I never knew of Larry losing a single case.

One evening, as I was leaving the ICU after making rounds, I met Larry in the hall. He was on his way to the operating room, and unlike most surgeons on the verge of performing surgery, he was grinning ear to ear.

"Hey, doc," he said, "Want to see an interesting case?"

"What's the case?" I asked.

"Aneurysms," he answered. "A head full of them. The angiogram looks like she could have bled from two of them, but I can see at least three more that haven't ruptured. If I can get to all five, it would break my record."

Five aneurysms? Now that was a surgery I couldn't miss. So I gowned up and watched as Larry gleefully clipped all five aneurysms, and, as always, the patient did well.

For Larry Franks, operating on five aneurysms was child's play, and it was that same childlike enthusiasm for so many things in his life— from the simple to the sublime—that I consider his most endearing quality.

Not only was Larry a wonderful neurosurgeon, but he was also a wonderful friend, and had it not been for Larry, that period of my life would have been far grimmer than it turned out to be.

CHAPTER 6: BART

When John Barton McMullan joined the Lovehandles, he was 36 years old, six feet tall, and weighed 150 pounds, exactly what he weighs today. With a wispy moustache and thick glasses, Bart fit today's picture of a geek to perfection. His appearance, coupled with a habit of clearing his throat before speaking, an accent that was unapologetically Southern, and speech that was sprinkled with words like "kaint" instead of "can't" and expressions like "he'd slap you upside the haid" could give those unfamiliar with Dr. McMullan the impression that he wasn't very smart.

But a longer encounter would produce a very different impression. In reality, Bart McMullan was a very intelligent man who knew exactly who he was and accepted himself as is. He was well aware of his idiosyncrasies, but he preferred to spend his time on things that were important to him rather than wasting it trying to change his image.

Bart was a very practical man. As long as things were serviceable, he would continue using them long after they were out of fashion. He continued wearing clothes he had purchased in high school and college as long as they were in reasonable condition. Despite a successful medical career, he chose to live in the same modest home that he and his first wife had purchased when they moved to Portland in 1972. After all, he reasoned, the house had a bedroom, a bathroom, and a kitchen—what more did you need?

He also had an uncanny ability to remember things according to where and when they happened, and he could recall the location, date, and time of every important event in his life. Likewise, he could stand in his living room and recite the purchase date and history of every item in it.

THE LOVEHANDLES

He cultivated useable skills and useful information. Although he allowed himself the pleasure of reading fiction, he alternated it with non-fiction in ratios that he thought would be conducive to both his entertainment and personal growth—and he kept a list of every book he read.

He spoke slowly and thoughtfully and corrected himself immediately if he said something that wasn't accurate. Despite this he was a good conversationalist and a wonderful storyteller, and had a charming self-deprecating manner. When his quirks were pointed out to him, he was the first person to laugh at them. Bart was just fine with being Bart.

Although I presented Tom Hoggard's story in the usual way—as a third-person narrative—here I'm changing the procedure. Because of Bart's exceptional memory for details and dates, as well as his penchant for storytelling, I have decided to let him tell his story in his own words, with very little help from me.

In January of 1979 I was at the yearly Adventist Hospital banquet when Tom Hoggard asked me to join his band. He said that Bob Crumpacker played the drums, he played guitar, and a girl named Patti was the singer. We talked, but I didn't commit. I said I'd have to think about it. Two weeks later he asked me again, and this time I said yes.

Although I was attracted to Patti right away, I played with the band for four months before asking her out. I took my time because my ex-wife, Susan, and I had just filed for divorce the year before, and I was in no hurry to get involved with someone new. I didn't find the waiting too hard, at least at first, but by the Friday after Memorial Day—a little more than four months after I'd met her—I was done waiting, and I asked Tom for her phone number. That was on June 1, 1979.

When Susan and I split, it was sudden and complete. Although the divorce wasn't final until January of 1979, once we decided to end it, the marriage was finished. She took her stuff and I took mine, and except for exchanging a few notes telling the other person to pick up something they left behind, we didn't even communicate. We would have been married eleven years that November.

But just like Patti, Susan and I met through music. There was this kid named Doyle McKee at my high school who, like me, played saxophone in the school band. He was a year younger than I was, and he wanted me and my brother to meet his new girlfriend, whose name was Susan. He said she was real cute, and he took us out to the high school to see her. It was summer, and Susan was playing tennis. As soon as I saw her, I thought, "Wow, I could really like that girl," but then I didn't do anything because she was going out with Doyle. But a couple of months later, this other kid named Tommy Finklestein, who also played saxophone in the high school band, started going out with her.

Tommy was a really good saxophonist, and went on to get a music degree from Louisiana State University and teach music. But Tommy and I were close personal friends, and I thought that if I asked Susan out it would mean the end of our friendship—just like I thought that dating Patti would break up the band. But finally I said to hell with it and asked Susan out, and just like I thought would happen, it chilled my relationship with Tommy forever. After that we were cordial, but never the friends that we were before. When Susan and I started dating—which was in October of 1958—I was the third saxophonist she'd gone out with. I guess she had a thing for saxophone players. (laughs)

Susan was a very attractive girl, and like Patti she had an unusual energy, a spark that made her different from other girls. When we began dating, she was fourteen and I was sixteen, and except for a couple of short breaks, we dated steadily through high school. Then I went away to Ole Miss [University of Mississippi], and when I was a junior she entered Ole Miss as a freshman. But we only had that one year together before I went to medical school. I graduated from college after my junior year; I'll tell you why in a minute.

The undergraduate school in Oxford and the medical school in Jackson were 160 miles apart, and seeing each other became a problem. Finally, Susan said she wanted more freedom, and we parted ways. It was her decision, not mine, and it hurt me a lot.

THE LOVEHANDLES

Then she married a guy named John who'd been a friend of ours in high school. She'd been studying to be a pharmacist, and they got married around the time she graduated. I only knew that because a friend of mine sent me a newspaper clipping about their wedding.

Then a month before I was to graduate from medical school, I got this letter from Susan. It was out of the blue; I hadn't seen or talked to her in over three years. The letter began, "I hear you're going to Thailand"—which wasn't true because I'd been in Thailand the summer before—but it went on to say that she was working in the Oxford Hospital pharmacy while John was studying for his MBA, and she hoped I was doing well. And that was it. I scratched my head and said to myself, "Now what in the hell was that about," because she was telling me something and I didn't know what.

But that letter stirred something in me. I thought I was over her, but I guess I really wasn't. So I called her at the hospital and said I could come up to Oxford on Saturday, and she said okay.

The trip from Jackson to Oxford took three hours. She was working, but we spent a couple of hours talking in the hospital pharmacy. It was clear that her marriage wasn't working out for a lot of reasons, but John had just gotten his MBA and taken a job in Jackson, and they would be moving there soon. So I let it go at that.

Then she called me after they'd moved. Although I'd graduated from medical school, I still had a month before starting my internship in Dallas. She said that John was in New Orleans for a couple of days, and could she see me that afternoon? It was an awkward time for me because I was dating two other women, and one of them was a girl named Marianne who I had known since grade school, and who was now teaching home economics in Vicksburg, Mississippi. I really liked Marianne, but I went to see Susan anyway. We talked for a couple of hours. It was clear that she was very unhappy with her marriage, but we didn't make any plans for the future. But a couple of days later she called me back and said she wanted to meet with me again.

This time we met in a department store parking lot. It was in the middle of the day and very hot. We were sitting in my car talking, and

52

I said, "So what do you want to do?" She said she wanted to leave John and get a divorce, and I thought, okay, that should be easy enough. But that was before I knew that short of murder it was impossible to get a divorce in Mississippi. Of course it's not that way now, but that was 1967. So I said, "Why don't you divorce John and move to Dallas? We can live together, and if it works out we'll get married."

Although that seemed reasonable to me, Susan suddenly burst into tears, jumped out of the car, and began running across the parking lot. When I got her back in the car she said, "I'm scared, I'm not sure what you mean, and I don't know what to do." So I calmed her down and promised that we'd talk later. Things had gotten complicated, and I had to think it over.

But when I thought about it some more, it seemed clear that she needed more reassurance than what I had given her. So the next day I called her back and said, "Look, if you divorce John and move to Dallas, we'll get married," and she accepted that.

Then I called a lawyer friend of mine and asked him how you went about getting a divorce, and he said that short of catching your spouse in the act of adultery, it was impossible to get a divorce in Mississippi. Well, Susan wasn't going to catch John committing adultery, so what were we going to do?

But then Susan found a lawyer who could get her a Mexican divorce. He would arrange everything and Susan could just go to Juarez and make everything final. But it would cost eight hundred dollars. and at that time neither one of us had any money. Then I remembered that the American Medical Association (AMA) was loaning money to young doctors for their internships and things like that, so I wrote them a letter saying that I needed eight hundred dollars for my internship, and the AMA sent me a check. The AMA loaned me money under false pretenses for a Mexican divorce. (laughs)

By then I had moved to Dallas, but before going to Mexico Susan stopped there to see me. Although I couldn't leave my internship to go with her, we spent some time together in the airport between her flights. Then she flew to Juarez and got the divorce. I guess it was pretty sleazy, but it was official, and that was all we needed. I've still got the papers, which have all sorts of ribbons and seals on them. Then we moved her stuff to Dallas and were married in November.

The first five years of our marriage were good. Those years covered my internship and the years I was in the Navy. But even then, every so often there would be an incident. The other night I had occasion to remember one that happened in 1969, after Susan and I had been married two years.

I remembered it because later this week I'm going back to Jackson for my fiftieth medical school reunion, and I wanted to recognize my old classmates. So I was looking through some of the fifty-five-millimeter slides I'd taken at the time. Then when I was done looking at pictures of my class, I thought I'd look through the pictures I'd taken of Marianne, who I'd been dating at the time. But when I couldn't find her pictures, I remembered why.

It happened when I was in the Navy and stationed in Charleston, South Carolina. One night I came home after work and the house was filled with smoke. I didn't know where the smoke had come from until I saw that right in the middle of the living room floor there was a trashcan where there'd recently been a fire. When I asked Susan what was going on, she said that she'd just burned all my pictures of Marianne, and I said, "You've done what?! Why in the world would you burn my pictures of Marianne?" I couldn't believe that she would do that. At the time Marianne was living somewhere in Tennessee and was no threat to anyone, especially Susan. But sometimes Susan would have these fits and do things like that. It was just the way she was.

But after we moved to Portland in 1972 for my residency, things changed for the worse and our marriage got real stormy. I was gone most of the time, and Susan was unhappy with that and said she wanted to be free—that there must be something or somebody out there that could make her happy besides me. So for a year and a half we separated and saw other people. Then we got back together and things were good for another three years. But when it fell apart again, we'd both had enough and decided to split.

Living alone was hard. For the first six months I was just going to work and not thinking about anything else. I couldn't plan anything. It was like I was in emotional shock—sort of like I am now. It wasn't until the first of the year that I even began thinking about another relationship, so it was a coincidence when Tom asked me to play in the band.

By January of 1979 I had begun to think that there might be a life ahead of me after all, and had started dating again. Even so, when I met Patti I was in no hurry to do anything. I was already seeing someone else, and I was afraid that if Patti and I started going out and we didn't get along that could cause trouble for the band. The band was probably the biggest reason I didn't call her. But the more I thought about her, the more I wanted to ask her out until I finally said, "To hell with the band! If it goes under, it goes under. (laughs)

On the Friday after Memorial Day I called Tom and got Patti's telephone number, and around 5:30 p.m. I called her. I'd been thinking about her a lot, but I don't think she'd been thinking about me. The reason I say that is because when she answered the phone and I said, "This is Bart," she said, "Bart who?" and I had to explain that I was Bart McMullan from the band. Then when I was talking to her about going out, I began by suggesting times in the future, and all at once she said, "Why not tonight?"

I said okay, but first I had to go to the hospital and see a patient that Erwin Syphers [a surgeon at Adventist] had asked me to see—a woman with a bad headache—so I could probably pick her up around 8:30 p.m., and Patti was fine with that. I went to see the patient, who turned out to have temporal arteritis. When she became a regular patient of mine, I always thought of her as "my Patti lady."

That night Patti and I went to Victoria Station, a restaurant that was made from an old train car and had really good prime rib. Then we came back to my house and had a few Irish coffees and talked until it was light outside. I can't remember what all we talked about, but she told me about Alan Beard and their breakup and all that. Then we discovered that we both had a knack for remembering things according to the year they happened, so we spent a lot of time telling each other about things we'd done during certain years in the past. It was a great night.

After she left, I sent her a dozen yellow roses. That impressed her. I'd always liked yellow roses, but some time after that I learned that yellow roses just meant friendship, so it was probably best that neither one of us knew what they meant. (laughs)

Band practice for the next week had been canceled because Bob or Tom had something else to do, so Patti and I went out to eat again, and this time we brought her daughter, Amy, along with us. Not too long after that, the three of us began living in my house on the weekends. Then when she and Alan Beard sold their condo, and Patti had moved into a smaller apartment, we stayed at her place on weekdays.

In late September I asked her to marry me, and she said she wasn't ready. She said that marriage was scary because of the experience she'd had with her first husband. A few weeks went by and I asked her again, but she still couldn't say yes. Finally, in late October we were having lunch at the Brasserie Montmartre, and I said, "Patti, I promise I won't ask you this again, but will you marry me?" And this time she said, "Yes," and that was that. Or at least that's what I thought.

But before we got married the question became, "Where were we going to live?" which was the last thing I thought would be a problem. My idea was that when the lease on her apartment ran out, she'd just move all her stuff into my house. But it wasn't going to be that easy.

There were some other issues, too. For instance, once we were married I thought she would take my name, but her answer to that was, "Oh, I thought you were going to change your name to Dunahugh!" In other words, "Why did you think I would change my name to yours when you won't change your name to mine?" I'd never thought of it that way, but it made sense. So I told her she could keep her name and I'd keep mine, and that was okay.

Then I asked her to sign a prenuptial agreement, and that conversation didn't go any better than the one about changing her name. She said that if I wanted to marry her it would be without a prenuptial agreement. So I dropped that, too.

But the thing about the house hung on, and that really puzzled me. Here I had this great house in a great part of town, and all she had to do was move in. But she wouldn't do it. She said either we had to sell the house or we'd have to completely redo it. To me that seemed unreasonable. When I asked her why, she said, "Because right now it's Susan's house, and I'm not living in Susan's house." But I said, "That's not true! A house is just a house, and besides that, we've been living here on weekends for a long time." And she still said no. But the more I thought about it, the more I realized that what she was saying wasn't so unreasonable after all. So finally I said okay, she could remodel the house.

The remodel started out easy enough. Patti's ex-husband, David, was an architect, and someone in his office drew up the plans. The biggest change would be moving the west wall out another eight feet, which would give us enough room for a large master bedroom and a separate bathroom for Amy. But there would be changes throughout the entire house.

But there was a problem. I'd been paying Susan off each month and didn't have any extra money. We needed a loan, but at that time there weren't any loans to be had. The prime rate was up to 21%, and basically the banks weren't lending money. Finally I went to First State Bank where I had all my accounts, and told them that unless I got a loan at a decent rate I'd move everything to another bank. They gave me a loan at 12%.

We were married in January of 1980. It was here at the house, and the only guests were my parents, Patti's mom—her dad had died when she was fourteen—my friend Bill Shoemaker, and his girlfriend, Nancy. There were thirty people at the reception, but no one from the band. We just wanted to keep it small.

Although the remodeling was supposed to start right after the wedding, it didn't begin until May. Even when things finally got going, nothing was happening very fast. Our problem was that the house had to be finished by the first of July, when Patti's lease ran out, so that she and Amy could move in. Although the contractor kept telling us that everything would be done on time, when the first of July rolled around, the house wasn't ready—not even close! In fact, there were no finished walls on the upper level, and the house was totally open. We had to farm Amy out to friends, and Patti and I moved into the basement. By the time the house was finished, Patti was so pissed off at the contractor and me that she was hardly speaking to either one of us. It was a tough way to begin a marriage, but we got through it.

I was born in Newton, Mississippi on September 5, 1942. Newton is a little town of two thousand people that's 65 miles east of Jackson and 30 miles west of Meridian. It's in the central part of the state, but a little bit to the east. In those days Newton was so small that it didn't have a stoplight. It does now, but it didn't then. Then when I was almost fourteen, my parents moved to Meridian, which had a population of fifty thousand and was the second biggest city in the state.

In the 1940s and 1950s, Newton was a place where no one ever locked anything. And there weren't any TVs, so we were always outside making Chinaberry bows and having BB gun fights. It was hot, but you got used to it. And there were chiggers, but you got used to them, too. No one wore shoes in the summer, so you had to toughen up your feet in the spring so you could stand to walk on the pavement.

When the DDT trucks came down the street, we'd run behind them and breathe in the poison air. Our parents didn't like that, but most of the time they didn't know what we were doing.

Ice trucks delivered ice twice a week. My family had a refrigerator, but a lot of folks didn't and they depended on those ice deliveries. The icehouse was really important to our town, because if you didn't have a refrigerator and you didn't have ice you couldn't survive the summers. It got *that* hot.

But besides the heat and the chiggers, Newton was an ideal place to grow up. It was safe so you could play anywhere. I don't think there's any place like that in America today, and looking back, it was a great place and a great time to grow up.

Of course, the South was segregated, but as a kid you didn't know what that meant. You knew there was a black section of town, but you never thought about it because that was just the way it was. The first time I thought about segregation was in the summer of 1954 when I was twelve years old. I remember that my mother ran out into the back yard and started yelling. She was upset and said that the Supreme Court had just ruled that we had to go to school with them. She probably used another word instead of "them," but I can't remember what she said. To my brother and me it didn't mean anything, but to my parents it obviously meant a lot.

On my fourth birthday, something happened to me. I remember standing in my bedroom in front of my chest of drawers and thinking, "I'm tired of this bullshit, and I'm the boss now." Of course back then I didn't know what those words meant, but what I felt was that I was as good as any adult, and from then on I was in charge of my own life. And as a four-year-old, I had condensed all that into "I'm the boss now"— but it meant the same thing.

I don't know why I felt that way, but it was a revelation to me, and it changed my life. And how I came to that opinion, I don't know. There was no abuse in my family, I had a fairly middle-class childhood, and I was a happy kid. But after that, it was a wonder that my parents didn't kill us, my brother and me.

My brother Dick was fourteen months younger than me, and by himself he was a sweet, well-mannered kid. Together, though, we were devils. One time we let twenty chickens loose in the house, and you can imagine what kind of mess that made. My dad had bought the chickens and put them in coops next to the house—I suppose we were going to eat them—but my brother and I took them into the house and let them loose. Then I set my brother's hobbyhorse on fire, and on Easter he and I threw raw eggs at each other in the living room.

When we got a puppy, my brother and I had an argument about whose puppy it was. Our mom said that we each owned half the puppy, so to make a point (I probably wouldn't have done it!) I got out a saw and said I was going to cut the puppy in half, right down the middle.

And my mom just lost it. We were like Dennis the Menace on steroids. We were always getting switched and having our privileges taken away, but I never complained because we deserved it.

It was just that I disagreed with my parents, especially my dad. It was like I refused to accept the beliefs that they thought I should have. We rarely got into arguments about it; we just held different opinions. In the end, I could only talk to my parents about certain things, but never about the things that were important to me. And when I left for college, I knew we'd never agree on anything that mattered.

Eventually we had a sister. She was born ten years after me. Although my brother and sister were younger than me, they're both dead now. My brother died at fifty-nine of ALS—Lou Gehrig's disease—and my sister died at sixty. I don't know why she died, exactly, but she was an alcoholic. In Mississippi you went to jail for DUIs, and because of that she had spent three years in jail. Maybe longer. When she got out, I tried to support her. I bought her a car and sent her money. She always sounded okay when she'd call, but I'm pretty sure she was still drinking. Patti would talk to her and suggest things she could do to make her life better, but it never helped. They found her dead in her mobile home. The autopsy said she died of a heart attack, but it was more likely due to the alcohol.

When my dad got out of the Navy after World War II, he started out in the banking business. I think he was president of the Newton County Bank. Then he started the Dodge-Plymouth dealership in Newton, but when we moved he sold that and bought the Chrysler dealership in Meridian. Around the time I finished high school, things went bad for him, and he lost the business. When I entered medical school, my parents moved to Mobile, Alabama, and my dad became the vice president of a bank there. After that, he and a partner started buying small businesses, including a phone company. My dad and I were cordial to each other but never close, and I never asked him about his businesses.

My mom began as a typical stay-at-home Southern mom, but after we started school, she worked as a tutor teaching Spanish, and after that she worked at my father's car dealership keeping the books. I got along with her better than I did with my dad simply because I knew she wasn't going to fight with me. When she was about sixty, she went to work at my uncle's furniture store and really loved it. She was a very outgoing person who liked to talk. Whenever my mother and Patti got together on the phone or we were down there visiting, I never said a word because they did all the talking. It was fun to watch. My mom worked at the furniture store for ten years before retiring.

My dad died when he was seventy-four, and my mom died when she was seventy-five. Both my parents were heavy smokers—Chesterfields. The house was always full of smoke.

I started playing the clarinet in the Newton Junior High School band when I was eleven or twelve. I played the clarinet for six months before I started playing the saxophone. I remember that my dad and I had this big brouhaha when I wanted to play the saxophone, probably because it was so expensive. My brother played the cornet. We never took private lessons because the band director taught us how to play. I played in the concert band and the marching band in both Newton and Meridian.

Meridian had the best high school band in Mississippi, and we won several contests in the three-state area. Our band director was a perfectionist and a taskmaster. He was an Italian named Eli Pacetti, a volatile guy who would just go crazy if you did something wrong. For instance, if you were in the marching band and weren't standing in quite the right spot, he'd come over and slap you upside the head and then jump up and down cursing at you. In the concert band, he might throw his baton at you if you hit a wrong note. He was very good, and as a result, we were very good. But if he did those things today, he'd be locked up.

When we were marching, I was the drum major—the leader of the band. But in the concert band, I just played alto sax. It wasn't until I was in Hoggard's band that I bought a tenor sax. The tenor is bigger, it's in a lower key, and it's the saxophone that's played in rock-and-roll bands.

THE LOVEHANDLES

In high school, there were five or six of us who got together and formed another band called the Lancers. This was *our* band, not a school band. There was another saxophonist in the Lancers, and we did this routine of synchronized movements with our horns. We thought it was pretty cool. The band wore identical jackets with spangles on them, and we got paid forty dollars a night playing for school dances after the football games.

In college I played with another band, but I can't remember its name. Maybe it didn't have one. The leader was the drummer, Curt Ayers. Besides Curt there were four or five other guys in the band. "Fats" Fitzgerald played the keyboards. He was this tall, good-looking guy with almost platinum hair, and the girls loved him. In college we got paid 135 to 145 dollars a job.

My divorce from Curt's band came over the Christmas holiday. The gig we were supposed to play was in Canton, Mississippi. Canton was about a hundred miles from Meridian, and because we were all from different towns, we had to furnish our own transportation. But my father and I had gotten into it, and he wouldn't let me have the car. So I said to hell with it and called Curt's home to tell him that I couldn't come. But Curt wasn't home, so I told his mother to tell him that I couldn't come, but she never gave him the message. When the band arrived in Canton and I was missing, Curt got all pissed off, and when he got back home, he was still mad and told me I was fired. I couldn't believe it. I told him I had asked his mother to tell him that I couldn't come, but at first he didn't believe me. Then when he asked his mom, she said that I'd called, and he apologized and invited me back into the band. But by then I had lost my desire to play in the band and said no.

I played in the concert and marching bands at Ole Miss, too, but just during my freshman year. I wanted to get through college in three years instead of four, so I was carrying a heavy schedule and couldn't afford the time. But I still played in the dance band, at least until Curt fired me.

Although I had already made the decision to go to Ole Miss, what I didn't know was that every year a man by the name of Carrier—like the air conditioner company—gave out a dozen scholarships for kids to go to Ole Miss. It was nothing that you applied for; the Carrier people would do all the research and just show up at your door to offer you a scholarship. And it was a great scholarship. Everything was pretty much paid for, the only requirement being that you went to Ole Miss.

So one day during my senior year of high school there was a knock on the door, and when I opened it, this wonderful gentleman named George Street was standing there to offer me a scholarship. It was probably a good thing, too, because at that time my father was having business problems and might not have been able to send me to college. The scholarship was for four years no matter what, so if I graduated from Ole Miss in three years instead of four, I could carry the scholarship over to my first year of medical school, which was why I wanted to get through college in three years.

I was a good student in college. I made all As except for a B in calculus—or maybe it was a C—and a B in judo. I understood the grade in calculus, but I couldn't believe that I got a B in judo. Some son of a bitch threw me down on the mat so hard that it broke my collarbone. Then when I asked the instructor why he gave me a B, he said it was because I broke my collarbone and couldn't wrestle. I could have killed him. (laughs)

A medical education in those days was a lot cheaper than it is now. Back then my medical school was only 750 dollars a year and I got through it cheap. The Carrier scholarship paid for my first year, I got jobs during the summers, I worked for a physiologist during the school year, and the Navy paid for my last year.

It was during the Vietnam War that the Navy was offering medical students a special deal. If I joined the Navy while I was in medical school, then during the last nine months of school I would be considered on active duty and get paid like an ensign—which was the same as an Army second lieutenant. The only catch was that if I did that, then I had to give the Navy an extra nine months. Then when I decided to go to submarine school, I agreed to give them another six months. So when I finished medical school it didn't cost my parents a thing and

THE LOVEHANDLES

I was only in debt four thousand dollars, but I had to serve three and a half years in the Navy. I actually gave them three years and nine months, but I didn't regret a second of it. I learned more during my time in the Navy than I did at any other equivalent time in my life, and the things that I learned were invaluable. It ended up being more than worth the time it cost me.

When I first began thinking about a career, I thought I was going to be a Presbyterian minister. But after reading books about the bible and what it took to be a minister, I thought, "That's bullshit." If I was a minister, I'd have to be nice to everyone all the time, and I'd be damned if I was going to do that. So that was the end of my plan to become a minister. (laughs)

In high school I was into science and thought I wanted to be a nuclear physicist, so to test that idea I applied for a National Science Foundation scholarship to study science at Louisiana State University between my junior and senior years. I got the scholarship, and at first I was put in with all these engineers, but as best I could tell, they were all capping out between thirty thousand and thirty-five thousand a year, which I didn't think was all that much. Then I was put with these pure science guys—people like physicists and chemists—and they seemed to spend most of their time sucking around trying to get grants from the government, and even after all their groveling, they weren't making that much either.

So when I finished my fellowship, I went back to high school and thought, "Well, what else can I do?" It was then that I began thinking about becoming a doctor.

The idea of becoming a doctor was totally analytical. I'd never even known a doctor. But I thought that if I became a doctor, I could earn a reasonable income, I wouldn't have to be nice to people if I didn't want to, I wouldn't have to suck around to get grants, and I could live any place I wanted—and what could be better than that? Although I didn't know anything about medical school, doctors seemed to have all the right options, so I applied to medical school.

And as it turned out, I had everything that medical schools were looking for. I'd done well on the MCAT test, and except for calculus and judo, I had all As. I had pretty much made it on those two things alone. So I got in. It was a pretty cold-blooded way to become a doctor, but I was good at medicine, and even though I had no grand notions about helping mankind, I did enjoy taking care of people.

CHAPTER 7: PATTI

Patti was an attractive woman: a tall, willowy brunette with big dark eyes, delicate features, and a smile that could melt your heart. She was smart, playful, and funny, but if circumstances demanded it, she would fight you to the death. Although she was naturally generous and compassionate, life had taught her to be wary, especially of men. She was a talker whose words could enchant you or cut you to shreds. She laughed readily, loudly, and with a very unladylike cackle, and if she was ever intimidated by anyone or anything, I never saw it.

Patti Pitts was born on April 3, 1945, in Cedar Rapids, Iowa, the fourth and final child of Marian and Edwin Pitts. Her oldest sibling, George, was nine years her senior, followed by Suzy, who was two and a half years older, and David, who was one year older.

Patti's childhood was tough. Her father was an alcoholic—a quarrelsome and abusive man whose wife kicked out of the house when Patti was ten. But without her husband's income, Mrs. Pitts struggled to support the family. Although she found a job assembling communication electronics at Collins Radio Company, one of Cedar Rapid's largest employers, her salary was barely enough to pay for the family's basic needs. Except for George, who was already in the Air Force, the other kids worked after school and on Saturdays to pay for their clothing, entertainment, and gas.

Four years after being ousted from the household, Mr. Pitts claimed to have stopped drinking and sought to rejoin the family. Working as a gas station attendant and supposedly sober, he described himself as a changed man, but the kids weren't buying it. Although Mrs. Pitts was anxious to reconcile, the children didn't want their father back. As hard as their lives were without him, they had been infinitely harder *with* him, and they argued against his return. The issue was still unsettled when Mr. Pitts died suddenly of a heart attack.

Patti was popular with the other students and enjoyed an active social life. During her sophomore year of high school, she began dating David Dunahugh, who was a year older and came from a wealthy family. A year before Patti was to graduate, David left Cedar Rapids to study architecture at the University of Oregon, but their feelings for one another remained strong, and they saw each other at Christmas and over the summer break.

After her high school graduation, Patti enrolled at the University of Iowa, but money was tight and she worked nights and weekends to remain in school. Then David proposed. Although a college education was important to Patti, she and David were in love and working to stay in school was difficult, so she accepted. They married the following summer and moved to Eugene, Oregon. Although their plan was that Patti would work while David finished school, then David would work while Patti went to school, after four years of marriage they decided to have a child, and in June of 1969, their daughter, Amy, was born.

Following David's graduation, he took a job with an architectural firm in Portland, and the Dunahughs relocated. Patti found a part-time job as a dental assistant and settled in for the long haul. But a year after moving to Portland, David began seeing another woman, moved out of the house, and sued Patti for divorce.

Thinking that David would be fair, Patti didn't contest the divorce, but when she discovered that all she would be getting was 135 dollars a month, she was furious. She returned to court seeking enough money for she and Amy to live on, but the judge ruled against her. That measly monthly payment was all she would ever get from David.

But if life had taught Patti anything, it was how to survive, and her job as a dental assistant had given her an idea. Compared to dental assistants, dental hygienists were paid very well, and if she became a dental hygienist, she and Amy could live comfortably.

Setting her sights on dental hygiene, Patti qualified for a federal education loan, and she and Amy moved into a small apartment within walking distance of Amy's school and near Mount Hood Community College, where Patti would be going to school. Two years later, she earned a degree in dental hygiene.

Patti found a job with a dentist whom she both liked and respected professionally, and suddenly she was making enough money for she and Amy to live on. It had been a struggle, but Patti was enjoying life again.

She began dating an architect by the name of Alan Beard, and when they started talking about marriage, they decided to test their relationship by buying a condominium together. Although Patti couldn't pay for half the condo, she contributed what she could.

But living with Alan and his two children brought out a side of Alan that she didn't like, and Patti wanted out of the relationship. The condo went up for sale, but when it sold, Alan refused to pay Patti for her part of the purchase. She took Alan to court, and this time the judge ruled in her favor.

Free of Alan Beard and his children, life was good again. Then one night her employer drank too much and died in a car crash, and Patti was out of a job.

But when another dentist bought the practice, Patti was again employed. Although she disliked her new employer intensely, characterizing him as a "cheapskate asshole," she had no choice but to continue working for him until she could find something better.

Finding something better would prove difficult, however, and the best she could do was cobble together three separate jobs: working two days a week with the dentist she detested, two days a week with another dentist that she liked, and one day a week teaching dental hygiene at Mount Hood Community College. Although this involved a lot of driving, the arrangement worked, and Patti was again making enough money to support herself and Amy. So when a doctor by the name of Tom Hoggard called and asked her to sing in his band, she felt like her life was stable enough to accept his offer.

Then the community college where she was teaching lost funding for her part-time position, but on the same day that her job there ended—June 1, 1979—Patti went on her first date with Bart McMullan.

THE LOVEHANDLES

Throughout the summer, Patti looked for a dentist who needed a full-time hygienist until she finally found one. Then Bart asked her to marry him, and after working through her fear of marriage brought on by her experience with David, she said yes. Professionally and personally, Patti's life was back on tract, and this time it would stay there.

Patti's earliest musical experiences were singing with her sister, Suzy. Both girls had nice voices, and they sang together at every opportunity. Then Patti took piano lessons, and though the lessons ended when her parents separated, she had learned enough to accompany herself and Suzy when they sang together. The girls joined the Sweet Adelines, a worldwide organization of women dedicated to singing barbershop harmony, and they sang in the church choir. Then in high school Patti found a group of girls who liked to sing, and joined them whenever possible.

After high school her singing was limited to informal situations, such as singing at parties or when friends dropped by, but she never lost the desire to sing in more organized situations—whether choirs, choruses, barbershop quartets, or bands like ours—and she collected sheet music to her favorite songs for the time when that would happen.

Although Patti had arrived in Hoggard's basement with the confidence of someone who had been singing with bands all her life, I was surprised to learn that she had never sung with a band before. Patti's confidence had come from her own life, where she had overcome challenges far tougher than singing with a couple of guys like us— which, in comparison to what she'd gone through, must have felt like child's play.

CHAPTER 8: THE BAND TAKES OFF

1. October 1979—Ed and Marie Kuehnel's Party
2. December 1979—George and Jean Sample's New Year's Party

In September of 1979, I received a letter with a return address that I didn't recognize. I tore it open to find an invitation to a party at the home of Ed and Marie Kuehnel on Summit Drive, a street in Portland's West Hills not far from mine. Although the invitation had been printed, a handwritten note at the top said, "Congratulations! We heard you've moved into the neighborhood." Now very interested, I studied the card more carefully and saw a line at the bottom that read, "Musical instruments welcome."

Ed Kuehnel was another young doctor who practiced at Adventist Medical Center. Ed was a nephrologist, a doctor who specialized in treating hypertension (high blood pressure) disorders of the kidneys, and electrolyte (sodium and potassium) disturbances. Since these problems often occurred in the sickest patients, Ed could frequently be found working in the hospital's ICU. Originally from New York City, Ed was known around the hospital for his intelligence, his ability to work long hours without complaint, and his dry sense of humor.

When I saw that musical instruments were welcome, I wondered if that might be an opportunity for our band to play publicly. Although Ed wouldn't know Patti, he would certainly know Tom and Bart, and might have even invited them to the party. But when I called Tom and Bart, neither one had received an invitation. Damn. Then I wondered if the Kuehnels would be offended if I told them about the band. Would that be overstepping my rights as a guest? Maybe . . . but I decided to take the chance. There was a telephone number on the invitation next to the request to RSVP, so I called it.

THE LOVEHANDLES

A woman with a friendly voice and a strong New York accent answered the phone. I figured this was probably Marie.

"Hi," I said, "This is Bob Crumpacker. I just got an invitation to your party and would love to come! Thanks for inviting me."

We talked for a while and then I popped the question, though not very gracefully. "I saw the line at the bottom of the invitation about musical instruments being welcome, and, uh . . . uh . . . well . . ."

"Bob, are you trying to tell me that you play a musical instrument?" Marie asked, laughing.

"Well, sort of," I said. "And I'm probably violating the rules of etiquette by mentioning this, but I play in a band with Tom Hoggard and Bart McMullan, who are both doctors at Adventist, and . . ."

"Bob," she said, still laughing, "Ed and I are always interested in violating the rules of etiquette, so please bring the whole band. I'll send invitations to Tom and Bart just to make it official."

I could hardly believe it. We had a gig!

The Kuehnels' Party

We arrived early and set up our equipment in the Kuehnels' living room. Other guests would be bringing their instruments so we couldn't play long, which was fine since we didn't know many songs anyway.

I met Marie; she was very nice and very chatty. We waited until the party had filled out a little, and then we played our songs. I think one or two couples danced, probably out of courtesy, and I can't recall any applause or requests to play more. Although it had been a very subdued beginning to our fabulous musical career, at least no one had thrown anything or told us that we sucked. We left our instruments, and some of the other guests got up and played.

I began mingling. I knew a few of the guests, and we passed some time chatting. Then I went into the kitchen and fixed myself a drink. A joint was being passed, and I took a hit or two. Then a young woman came into the kitchen asking for me. She said her name was Cheryl and she had a question.

"Ask away," I said.

"What area of the brain is damaged in an expressive aphasia?" she asked.

"Wow," I said, "that's a pretty strange thing to ask someone at a party."

She said it was a test. Someone wanted to know if I was really a neurologist.

"It's Broca's area," I said.

Cheryl laughed and said, "Okay, I guess that makes you a neurologist," and walked away.

I topped off my drink and went into the living room. I was feeling pretty good and talked to a lot of people. Then I saw Cheryl standing beside a young woman with wild red hair. I walked over to her and asked if she was the one who wanted to know.

"Wanted to know what?" she asked.

"If I was really a neurologist," I said.

"Maybe," she answered, smiling. I thought that was pretty funny.

I told her my name was Bob, and she said her name was Caroline. Then she, Cheryl, and I talked for a while, but I kept looking at Caroline. There was something about her that I really liked. Maybe it was the hair, which looked like a big red afro. But she had a nice smile, too, and when we talked her blue eyes looked right into mine. We laughed, too—I can't remember why—and it just felt *good* being with her. Then she left and I talked to Cheryl, who told me that Caroline was a psychiatric nurse and that she was divorced. I said that I was divorced, too, and Cheryl just laughed and said that they already knew that.

Then Cheryl left to visit with some other folks, and I talked to some other people too. Everyone seemed to be laughing. It was a good party. Then Cheryl and Caroline came back, Cheryl said that it had been nice meeting me, and she left the party for good. Caroline and I continued talking, and I saw some people out on the porch passing another joint. I asked Caroline if she wanted to go out on the porch. She said she did.

When we came back inside, there were people in the living room doing acrobatics. Caroline did some cartwheels, and I stood on my head. Caroline tried to stand on her head too, but she was laughing so hard that she just kept falling over. More time passed and the laughing slowed down, but Caroline and I were still together. As the party was breaking up, I asked her if she wanted to see my house. She said she did. Maybe it was good that I had bought it after all.

Johnny Limbo and the Lugnuts

Shortly after Bart joined the band, Hoggard suggested that we go as a group to see a local band called Johnny Limbo and the Lugnuts. Tom said that they played rock and roll hits from the past and were very entertaining. We could do worse, he said, than to model our band after theirs.

Although we eventually saw Johnny Limbo and his crew several times, the first time they were playing to a packed house at a small basement bar in downtown Portland. The band had formed the previous year as a gag but had caught on and was quickly gaining a following.

In 1969 a rock and roll band called Sha Na Na played at the Woodstock music festival and appeared briefly in the documentary film *Woodstock*, right before Jimi Hendrix closed out the festival with "The Star-Spangled Banner." Formed by students from Columbia University in New York City, Sha Na Na wore gold lamé outfits and leather jackets, and had pompadours and ducktail hairdos. They performed songs and dance routines from the 1950s and parodied the music of early rock and roll. Sha Na Na caught on, and between 1977 and 1981 they hosted their own TV variety show, which was one of the most popular shows on television. And they're still playing today. Johnny Limbo and the Lugnuts were Portland's version of Sha Na Na.

Johnny Limbo and his band played nothing but rock and roll classics, and they played them well. Their front man, Johnny Limbo (real name Jerry Hofmann) sang lead and played the trumpet. The Lugnuts were a big outfit that featured a variety of instruments— keyboards, horns, and saxophones in addition to the usual guitars, bass, and drums—which allowed them to play a variety of rock and roll styles. In addition, the Lugnuts sang well enough to provide competent backup to Hofmann's lead.

But their most endearing quality was their showmanship. They were having a good time, and they wanted the audience to share in the fun. When Hofmann wasn't singing, he was constantly in motion, interacting with the audience, telling jokes, and pulling gags on various band members. They played most songs straight but parodied many, sometimes slipping into costume to poke fun at the greaser look of Elvis or the bad-ass biker style of "Born to Be Wild." In addition, the fun was all G-rated. Part dance band, part stage show, Johnny Limbo and the guys worked hard to show the audience a good time, and for us, watching them perform was time well spent.

Franks Talks Dirty

Larry Franks grew up in Mattoon, Illinois, a manufacturing town of fifteen thousand in the middle of the state. His mother was a homemaker, and his father was an industrial spring salesman. Larry decided to become a neurosurgeon when a neck injury left a football teammate paralyzed.

More than any doctor I have ever known, Larry Franks identified with the common man. Despite performing at an exceptional level in a very demanding profession, Larry never saw himself as more than another blue-collar guy.

The Willamette River divides Portland into eastern and western sections. The streets on the east side of the river are designated as either Southeast or Northeast, while those on the west side are either Southwest or Northwest. But in Portland, this east-west division is more than just geographic. Although there are numerous exceptions to this generalization, people who live on the west side of the Willamette River are more affluent than those on the other side. The corollaries to this are obvious: those who live on the west side of town go to better schools, are exposed to less crime, have better roads, dine at nicer restaurants, live in bigger homes, take better vacations, and so on.

Larry was well aware of these differences and took great pride in the fact that he was an east-side guy. And it was no coincidence that he worked at Portland Adventist Medical Center, which despite its recent upgrade continued to serve a very east-side demographic.

I think that one of the reasons that Larry and I bonded so easily was that he understood that those east-siders were my people, too. Although I was the son of a doctor, my father was raised on a farm and had passed his profound respect for the working class on to me. In addition, my own history as a paperboy, dishwasher, landscaper, baker, waiter, construction worker, security guard, fast-food cook, and oil field roustabout was strictly blue-collar, too. And like Larry, I was entirely at ease around working people and took great pleasure in trying to help them.

Although Larry hadn't yet moved to Portland when I was living in Lake Oswego, I think that he viewed my final move to the west side of town as a bit of a betrayal. Over time, though, he turned this into a series of jokes based on the supposed differences between our east- and west-side lifestyles. For example, if I were coming over to visit him, he might suggest that I put a rifle in my gun rack. When I reminded him that life on the west side was so safe that people didn't own guns and therefore didn't need gun racks, there would be a long pause after which he would say that although he still wanted to see me, he couldn't guarantee my safety unless I was armed. On my first Christmas as a west-sider, his present to me was a sledgehammer. On another Christmas, it was a gigantic wrench.

One day Larry called to tell me something that he thought was funny. He had just seen a young man whom he had operated on for carpel tunnel syndrome—a common, straightforward, and easily treatable condition in which a nerve is pinched at the wrist. The patient had recovered from his surgery and was now free of his symptoms. But at the conclusion of his appointment, the young man had said, "Oh, doctor, doctor, doctor, thank you for taking care of my problem. God bless you!"

Unfortunately, I didn't understand what Larry thought was so funny about the man's overly effusive compliment. If anything, it seemed kind of pathetic. So I asked Larry what part of it he thought was funny.

Although he was disappointed that I didn't catch the humor right away, Larry explained that it was because the man had used the word "doctor" not once, but three times, as though the word carried so much weight that the more times it was said, the more respect it conveyed. And, of course, Larry thought that anything more than a simple "thank you" for something as easy as a carpel tunnel operation was ridiculous. He was just doing his job. No big deal.

"Okay," I said, still not seeing the humor. "Sorry. I guess I missed that."

But the next time Larry called me, he began the conversation with, "Oh, doctor, doctor, doctor, doctor, doctor. Doctor, doctor, doctor, doctor, doctor, doctor. DOCTOR, DOCTOR, DOCTOR! Oh, God bless you, doctor!" And this time I got it—and it really was funny.

A few weeks later, after he had rattled off another "doctor"-laden greeting, Larry became serious.

"Doctor," he said, "I'm very concerned. Recently, I've been having a disproportionate amount of gas with my stools. Instead of my usual ratio of 3.7 liters of gas per pound of feces, this past week I've been emitting 5.4 liters. Doctor, I find this very concerning. I've analyzed my diet, I've searched all the pertinent literature, and I've consulted the best specialists in the field, but no one can tell me what it means. Doctor, you're my last hope. Do you think I could be evaporating from the inside out?"

And the next time it was, "Doctor, do you have a minute to listen to a rather strange chain of events, and then tell me what you think it means?"

"I do," I said.

Larry continued, "So, doctor, two nights ago when I took off my underpants, I saw two parallel skid marks that formed a perfect equals sign. Equal to what, I wondered? Then last night, I was hoping to find some indication of what the equals sign was referring to, but when I checked my underpants, doctor, there was nothing there. No marks of any kind. Doctor, I'm confused. Do you think that instead of an equals sign, the marks were two negative signs, which of course would indicate a positive? But if that's true, then a positive *what?*"

Discussions of this type continued well past our respective retirements. To Larry, this was just another way of undercutting the medical profession's tendency to present doctors as something special. Larry found it hilarious that two supposedly learned physicians, one a neurologist and the other a neurosurgeon, could be discussing feces, flatus, and skid marks in a scholarly manner. And I guess I did, too.

Caroline, Bill, and Tim

Following the Kuehnels' party, my relationship with Caroline progressed rapidly. A few weeks after meeting her, I began spending nights at her home, which was only a couple of miles from mine. Caroline had two young sons, Tim, ten, and Bill, eight, who lived with her during the week and with their father and his wife on the weekends. Although the boys and I had been introduced and they knew that Caroline and I were dating, they had not been told I was sleeping there, too.

One weekday morning after Caroline had gone downstairs to fix the boys' breakfasts, her son Bill opened the door and walked into the bedroom looking for his mother. As soon as I heard the door open, I pulled the covers up over my head, hoping to escape detection. Calling her name, Bill tentatively approached the mound of bedcovers, under which I was doing my best to become invisible, and pulled the covers back.

I had had no experience with kids, and therefore I had no idea how to handle this embarrassing situation, so I smiled and said, "Hi, Bill. Your mom's downstairs making breakfast," as innocently and as matter-of-factly as I could.

A look of shock settled on Bill's face as he silently backed out of the room, closing the door behind him. I lay there feeling terrible, afraid that I had just inflicted irreparable damage to Bill's young psyche and ruined his life forever.

I stayed in the bedroom until the boys had left for school, then went downstairs. When Caroline greeted me with a smile and asked what I wanted for breakfast, I knew that Bill hadn't mentioned finding me in her bed. So I told her.

She was upset, but more with herself for not telling the boys that I was staying there at night than she was with what had just happened with Bill. She left the kitchen immediately to go upstairs and dress. When she came back down, she said that before work she would be going to Tim and Bill's school to explain to them why I was in her bed—well, not exactly why I was in her bed—but rather about the strong feelings that sometimes developed between a man and a woman that made them want to spend their nights together. Even though she presented her plan optimistically, I could tell that she was worried about their reactions. And since any adverse consequence of Bill's discovery could affect my relationship with Caroline, I was worried, too.

I shaved, showered, dressed, and left for work, but I couldn't keep my mind off the incident. But later that day Caroline called to reassure me that Tim and Bill had both accepted her explanation as well as the news that in the future we would be spending more nights together. And that sounded perfect.

Love Machine?

At a band practice shortly before the holidays, Bart and Patti announced that they would be getting married in January. That was a shocker. Prior to their announcement, I had observed nothing to make me suspect that they were romantically involved—no adoring glances, lingering touches, or words of endearment. Nothing. Nor had Tom, who Bart had called on June 1 to get Patti's telephone number, made the connection either. But in less than a year, the band had brought three of its four members into romantic relationships.

THE LOVEHANDLES

The Samples' New Year's Eve Party

Another one of Adventist's young lions was a pulmonologist by the name of George Sample. His last name was an Anglicized version of Zampaglione; the change having been made by George's Italian grandfather in the early 1900s. George grew up in the coal mining regions of Pennsylvania and West Virginia, and had been inspired by a local physician to become a doctor. He graduated from the George Washington University School of Medicine in Washington, DC, and had just begun an internal medicine residency at the Harrisburg Hospital in Harrisburg, Pennsylvania, when he had a life-changing experience. After visiting a friend in Portland, George fell in love with the Pacific Northwest, and decided to finish his residency at OHSU. Coincidently, Tom, Bart, and future band member Les Naman were there at the same time.

George's specialty of pulmonology is an internal medicine subspecialty that deals with disorders of the lungs. Although the phrase "disorders of the lungs" makes pulmonology sound very limited in its application, it is anything but. Because pulmonologists are experts in managing mechanical ventilation, they are involved in the treatment of all conditions whose common denominator is an inability to breathe without mechanical assistance—that is, without a respirator. This includes not only patients with respiratory problems but also many patients with heart problems or nervous system problems as well. Although George had an office in Adventist's professional office building, most of the time he could be found in the ICU, keeping the hospital's sickest patients alive.

George was a tall, handsome guy whose sad, expressive eyes mirrored the worry and sleep deprivation that his job produced. At work, he was a conscientious and compassionate man who relentlessly pursued each medical problem through the ever-changing labyrinth of its own complications, but away from work, George was a charming and funny guy who loved a good party. And although I had never been to one of their affairs, he and his wife, Jean, were said to throw some of the best parties in town. Their annual New Year's event enjoyed almost mythical status in the medical community.

George and Jean heard about our band through the hospital grapevine and sent us an invitation to play at their New Year's party. We received the invitation with a mixture of joy and trepidation. Although it would be an honor to play for their party, in order to fill an entire evening with danceable music, we would need to learn a number of new songs and then come as close as we could to perfecting them. There was something about George that demanded the best, and we definitely felt the pressure to live up to that standard.

The band went to work and learned as much new material as we could, but by the time of the party, we still didn't have enough songs to fill an entire evening. Patti suggested that we play a few of the songs from our first set again in the second. Although this sounded a little chancy, we had no choice, and in retrospect I don't think anyone noticed.

We began playing to an empty dance floor, which remained that way for the first several songs—a terrifying situation for a dance band as new as ours. But between numbers, the ever-fearless Patti kept up a pleasant patter, introducing each new song and reminding passers-by that their lives would be so much better if they just danced, until finally the floor was filled with people dancing and having a good time. And when we finished and were packing up our equipment, a number of people came by to tell us how much they had enjoyed our music. Despite a shaky start, our first full performance had been a success.

A noteworthy aside is that by the time of Samples' party, Caroline and I had been dating for a couple of months, and in Caroline's honor, Patti decided that our opening number should be Neil Diamond's "Sweet Caroline." It remained our leadoff song for many years and continued on as a band staple after that.

The Lovehandles

Names

Most bands come into the world without names, but once a group of musicians has attained some sense of cohesion, it is time for them to select a name. Although there must be some bands that arrive at their name quickly and easily, that has never been my experience. Unless a band has a recognized leader who makes all their decisions, naming a band can be a long, difficult process.

The problem with picking a name is the number of criteria it must fulfill. Each musician wants the name of their band to be personally satisfying in a number of very different ways, many of them hard to define or even subconscious. Add to that the fact that no two band members have the same criteria, and you can see why choosing a name is difficult.

But some requirements for a name are universal. Since a band's name is its calling card, it must capsulize some aspect of your band's essential self. When people hear your band's name, they should immediately understand something of its true identity: who you are, what kind of music you play, or how you see the world. Once chosen, you must be comfortable with your band's name and be able to say it proudly. And above all, you should think that your band's name is cool.

In my experience, there is a method for selecting a band's name that has probably been around since people first gathered and slapped sticks together, pounded on rocks, or beat on hollow logs. As soon as a group of musicians recognize themselves as an entity, someone will say, "So, what should we call ourselves?" and the process begins.

Once that question has been voiced, the musicians, who have invariably been thinking about names for some time, will open up, and there will be a sudden outpouring of names for consideration. This will be followed by a long pause as each band member considers the offerings, and then the sorting process begins. Many of the names will be rejected outright, some quietly and some vehemently, others will be discussed, and a few will be filed away for extended consideration.

Then the subject will be dropped until the band convenes again, when there are more offerings, further discussion, and more extended consideration. This process will continue for a variable period of time during which arguments may erupt and feelings may be hurt. There is even a risk that in their search for a name, the musicians will find that they are not compatible, and there will be no band left to name.

Our particular selection process was influenced by the fact that we had already chosen Johnny Limbo and the Lugnuts as our role model. Tom had been the first member of the band to see them in concert, and he'd left convinced that they were a group worth emulating. And after seeing them for ourselves, we had agreed with his opinion. They were a cover band that people could dance to; they were fun, friendly, and entertaining. Our name would need to reflect those same qualities, and though that narrowed the field considerably, the process was still difficult.

I wish I could recall some of the names we went through before arriving at "The Lovehandles Band," or just "The Lovehandles," but I can't; it was too long ago. But when our eventual name was first suggested, I remember it arriving like a meteor and silencing all dissent in its path. And in the end, although the name didn't win complete, unequivocal approval, it was accepted by all as being good enough.

Who came up with the name? Well, I think I did, but I can't say that with certainty. In the past, when I've mentioned this to the rest of band, some have disagreed, saying that it was either their idea or someone else's idea. So maybe they're right and I'm wrong. It doesn't really matter. Whoever came up with "The Lovehandles" picked a pretty good name. It's funny, friendly, and conjures up an image associated with middle age—and that was who we were.

CHAPTER 9: LES

Les Naman was soft-spoken, generous, and kind—a gentleman in the truest sense. Of average height, slightly built, and prematurely gray, Les owned one of the most beautiful smiles to ever grace the planet.

Born on September 13, 1941, Leslie Rodney Naman was the firstborn son of wealthy parents. He became a doctor, married the daughter of an equally wealthy Pittsburgh industrialist, and between two marriages had three beautiful children. Yet beneath this glossy exterior, Les had a problem that he struggled with throughout his life.

Although some of this account comes from my memories of Les, most of it is the result of several conversations that I had with Les's first wife, Cheryl Woods, who knew him best.

Les's father, Evins Naman, was a successful California winegrower whose grapes sold to some of the country's biggest wineries—Christian Brothers, Carlo Rossi, and Gallo—as well as to the world's largest producer of raisins, Sun-Maid. The son of Armenian immigrants, Evins was handsome, charming, friendly, and so easygoing that if his plans— anything from dinners to vacations—were suddenly disrupted, he could shrug his shoulders and laugh about it.

At first glance, Evins's wife, Dorothy, was so different from her husband that without invoking the old saw that "opposites attract," it might be difficult to explain their attraction to one another. First of all, Dorothy was tall—five feet, ten inches—while her husband was only five feet, six inches. Second, in contrast to Evins's good looks and personal warmth, Dorothy was, plain, shy, and socially awkward, traits that could be blamed on the repeated eye surgeries she underwent as a child and the thick, unflattering glasses that she wore throughout her life. But despite these outward differences, Evins and Dorothy had a wonderful relationship and a strong marriage.

While they shared a love of friends, family, wine, cooking, gardening, and travel, each pursued their own separate interests. Besides managing his own wine business, Evins became the head of public relations for the Wine Institute and traveled throughout the state promoting the interests of California wine growers. He was also a frequent lecturer on enology—the study of wines—at Fresno City College.

Dorothy's interests took her in a very different direction. As a schoolgirl without the good looks or popularity that would assure her of marriage, she sought a career, and in so doing she fell in love with science. For most of her adult life Dorothy taught biology, chemistry, and physics at Fresno City College when most married women would never think of working outside the home. So strong was her passion for science that she once spent a year's sabbatical at the University of California, Los Angeles (UCLA) taking medical school science courses for no more than her own education and enjoyment. If she had been given the opportunity to teach at one of the state's larger and more prestigious institutions, she probably would have done so, but Dorothy taught in an era when women were largely excluded from faculty positions at major universities.

For the time in which they lived, the Namans were an unusual family. When Cheryl was first invited to their home for dinner, Les mentioned that his mother would not be there. His mother, he said, was living in Los Angeles and taking medical school courses at UCLA. When Cheryl asked if his mother were going to medical school, Les said no, she just liked science.

Les's mother was spending a year away from her home to attend science classes? Cheryl could hardly believe it. In contrast, Cheryl's mother had no intellectual interests. She had worked as a model prior to her marriage and after that became a housewife and stay-at-home mom.

Then when Les said that his father would be making their dinner, Cheryl was incredulous. Her own father was helpless in the kitchen, and she had never known anyone whose father cooked.

But as different as their families were, Cheryl's first dinner at the Namans' would become one of her fondest memories. Although Les's mother would be gone, his wise and witty grandmother, Araxie Naman, would be there in her place.

For the occasion, the Namans had spared nothing. The dinner table was covered with a starched white linen tablecloth; set with their best china, crystal, and silverware; and decorated with fresh flowers from their garden. But when Cheryl, in her nervousness, spilled her glass of red wine on the white tablecloth, she feared that she had spoiled the evening. But without missing a beat, Grandma Naman reached out and tipped over her *own* glass of wine so that Cheryl wouldn't feel uncomfortable—an act of kindness that Cheryl would never forget.

Les and Cheryl met at San Francisco General Hospital, where Cheryl was a nurse and Les was an intern. It was1967, the year of San Francisco's Summer of Love and Haight-Ashbury, the war in Vietnam, and the many protests that the war inspired.

Les's only sibling was his younger brother, Larry, and when Cheryl and Les first met, Les and Larry were living together. The difference between the two boys was striking. Les was clearly the golden boy, handsome and charming, while Larry—although he was a brilliant student—was short and homely, his face scarred with acne.

Then Larry began to change. He let his hair grow long and his hygiene lapse, and he became critical of traditional beliefs and institutions. Although rebellion was typical of the period, to those who knew him best, this seemed more like a change in Larry than it did a sign of the times. While attending San Francisco State College, Larry had met a girl by the name of Abby who shared his radical views, and when they both dropped out of school and moved to Oregon, Larry's parents worried about his mental health.

Although Les and Cheryl's romance was taking a more conventional course, Cheryl had noticed that at times, Les could be very forgetful. In fact, on their first date, Les had taken her to an expensive restaurant in San Francisco's Chinatown, but when it came time to pay, Les had forgotten to bring any money. Since Cheryl hadn't brought any money either and neither of them had any credit cards, the owner of the restaurant demanded that Les leave his Rolex watch as security. But after a good deal of talking, the owner was finally persuaded that Les was an honest man who would return to pay his bill—which he did.

Although Cheryl continued to witness examples of Les's forgetfulness, both she and Les were so busy at work that his forgetfulness seemed excusable. Soon Les and Cheryl were engaged, the wedding to take place at Cheryl's home in Pittsburgh shortly before the end of Les's internship.

In those days, blood tests for syphilis were required before a couple could marry. Les and Cheryl had taken their tests in San Francisco, and Les was to have brought the results with him to Pittsburgh to present to the minister. Although Cheryl was certain that Les would never forget something as important as their test results, just to be sure, she asked if he had brought them. But Les's when face fell, she knew that he had forgotten them.

Cheryl was stunned. How could he have done that? There would be 175 of their families' closest friends at the wedding reception—some who had traveled thousands of miles to be there—and what would she tell them if the minister refused to perform the ceremony?

In desperation Cheryl confided in her mother, who just smiled and told her not to worry. There was a doctor, her mother said, a good friend of theirs, who would fix the problem. Then she called the doctor and asked if he would be willing to do them a big, big favor. Of course, he said, whatever you need, and after hearing the story, the doctor wrote a letter to the minister saying that he had seen their test results himself—which, of course, he hadn't—and would vouch for their normalcy. Although disaster had been averted, Cheryl saw the incident as an ominous sign, and for the first time since meeting Les, she wondered if their love would be strong enough to survive his forgetfulness.

After the wedding, Les and Cheryl returned to San Francisco for Les to finish his internship and prepare for the Army. Because of the war in Vietnam, Les had signed up for the Berry Program, but he'd been informed by the Department of Defense that he would be entering the Army immediately after his internship—which was the same as being told that he was going to Vietnam. So when his internship ended, Les and Cheryl packed their car and drove to Fort Sam Houston in San Antonio, Texas, where Les would receive his basic training in preparation for deployment.

But at Fort Sam Houston, Les seemed more forgetful than ever, and although Cheryl had no idea what the trouble was, she urged him to see a psychiatrist. Les agreed, and after a few visits, the psychiatrist wrote a letter to Les's commanding officer saying that Les was unfit for overseas duty and should remain stateside to receive psychotherapy for the duration of his assignment.

Although Cheryl didn't know the nature of her husband's problem, she took the doctor's action to mean that Les had an emotional disorder that was serious enough to exempt him from Vietnam, and that worried her. Not only had Les's brother, Larry, been acting strangely, but other members of the Naman family had also been having problems. Evins's sister, Ethyl, had two boys, Phillip and Neil, who were both suffering from mental illnesses. Phillip had been diagnosed with schizophrenia, and although Neil would never receive a formal diagnosis, his behavior had become so bizarre that mental illness could be the only explanation.

After a normal early life, Neil had married and fathered two daughters, one blessed with a beautiful singing voice. When the girl was old enough to perform, Neil left his wife, while he and his daughter moved to Vancouver, Canada, where she supported him by singing on the street.

Cheryl knew that mental illnesses such as schizophrenia and bipolar disorder ran in families, but all she could do was hope that Les's problem, whatever it was, was not like those of Larry, Phillip, or Neil.

So instead of going to Vietnam, Les was sent to Fort Leavenworth in Leavenworth, Kansas. Although the post's doctors spent most of their time working at the medical clinic, they also took turns staffing the infirmary for the U.S. Disciplinary Barracks, the military's only maximum-security prison.

It was no secret that the doctors disliked working at the prison. Although the inmates were occasionally sick, most of the time they were feigning symptoms to get narcotics, avoid unpleasant tasks, or convince the judge that their crimes were really due to mental illness. But Les was so thankful not to be going to Vietnam that he volunteered to be the post's full-time prison doctor.

During his time at Fort Leavenworth, Les continued his psychotherapy with a doctor in Kansas City, driving the ninety miles to and from the doctor's office once a week. By the end of his two-year tour of duty, Cheryl thought he was emotionally stronger and urged him to continue his psychotherapy for another year. So following his discharge from the Army, they moved to Kansas City, where Les worked in an emergency room while he continued his therapy. Then after a year in Kansas City, Les and Cheryl moved to Portland, where Les began his three-year residency in internal medicine at OHSU.

Ever since Larry had dropped out of school, the Naman family worried about his mental health and had stayed in contact with him as much as they could. During Les's first year in the Army, Larry was still available by phone and even visited them at Christmas, but when Larry called to say that he and Abby were joining a commune and would no longer be reachable by phone, the family's concern increased. Then when months passed with no word from Larry, the four of them—Les, Cheryl, Evins, and Dorothy—decided to visit the commune.

Unfortunately, the directions they had been given didn't mention that the road to the commune was blocked by a river. Although they could see the commune on the other side, the only way to get there was by climbing into a rickety basket hanging from a rope, and pulling the basket across the river by hand. And to complicate matters, the basket was at that moment on the other side of the river.

With no way of crossing the river, they called Larry's name until he appeared and took the basket across to meet them. They talked for a while, and although Larry invited them to see the commune, the basket looked so dangerous that they just thanked him and left, their visit too brief to tell how Larry was doing.

Then in 1971, the year that Les and Cheryl were living in Kansas City, they got a call from Abby saying that she and Larry had left the commune and were living in Salem, Oregon—and that she was pregnant. When their daughter, Willow, was born, Larry and Abby brought her to Portland and stayed with Les and Cheryl for a couple of weeks. Although Larry was still acting strangely, it was reassuring that he had wanted to see them.

But in May of 1973, Les and Cheryl received a call from Abby saying that Larry had been committed to a mental hospital. He had come home with a loaded shotgun threatening to kill both her and Willow, but then he'd fallen on the floor sobbing. His family had rushed to the hospital to offer their help, but Larry now saw them as his enemies and vanished after his discharge from the hospital.

Because of Les's concern for his brother and the toll that Larry's disappearance was taking on their parents, Les never gave up trying to find his brother. Periodically he would have an idea about where Larry might be and go there to look for him—but never with any success.

Meanwhile, Evins and Dorothy had become so obsessed with Larry's disappearance that they could think of little else, and even when they were with Cheryl, Les, and their grandchildren, the conversation invariably turned to Larry, his problems, and his possible whereabouts.

Then Les received a tip from the U.S. Postal Service that a Larry Naman had been picking up mail at a tiny post office in rural Oregon. Although Les watched the post office for days, Larry never appeared.

Despite Larry's problems, Les and Cheryl seemed to be doing well in Portland. They had bought a beautiful house overlooking the city—the same house where Caroline and I were married—and they had two children, Monica and Seth. Les had completed his residency in internal medicine and taken a job with Kaiser Permanente. On the surface, Les and Cheryl appeared to be living happy, successful lives.

But Les's problems were continuing to strain their marriage. Although Les's forgetfulness was an ongoing issue, it was his emotional detachment from everything around him—Cheryl and the kids included—that Cheryl found the most troubling.

Finally, she could stand it no longer and told Les that she wanted a divorce, and just as she feared would happen, Les was heartbroken.

THE LOVEHANDLES

Cheryl felt terrible. Whatever was going on inside Les's head to make their marriage so difficult, it was nothing that he had any control over. Whether his issues were related to the mental illness that ran through his family or due to something entirely different, it wasn't his fault—not at all. In fact, Les was one of the sweetest, kindest men she had ever known, and in all the years that they had been together, they had never had a single argument—surely a record of some sort. But for her own well-being, she had to proceed with the divorce. But how, she wondered, could she make the divorce easier for Les?

Then Cheryl had an idea. Although she hadn't learned about his musical talent until after they were married, Les played the piano very well. And there was that doctor band that had played at the Kuehnels' party, and two of its members—Tom Hoggard and Bart McMullan—had done their residencies at OHSU at the same time that Les was there and probably knew him. And she had met the band's drummer, Bob Crumpacker, who was dating her best friend, Caroline. And if Cheryl asked Caroline to tell Bob that Les played the piano, and Bob told the band, and if the band was looking for a piano player and asked Les to join the band . . . maybe that would help Les get through the divorce. Although there were a lot of "ifs," "ands," and "maybes" to the plan, Cheryl thought it might work.

And it did. We liked Les immediately and were delighted to have him in the band, and in turn the band helped Les through the divorce. Although we were all aware of Les's forgetfulness, none of us knew its severity, and just as Cheryl had done at the beginning of their courtship, we thought it was little more than a funny and harmless idiosyncrasy. And even though it must have tormented Les, he never let on. In fact, when he told us stories about his forgetfulness, he did so laughing, as though he was having as much fun telling us the story as we were having hearing it.

My own introduction to Les's problem came one morning when Les had asked me to drive him to the airport. When I arrived at his home, he came down the steps promptly and put his suitcase in the trunk. But after getting in the car and buckling his seat belt, he remembered something else, unbuckled his seat belt, and left the car saying he would be right back. Then he returned with another piece of luggage, stowed it in the trunk, got back in the car, and buckled up again. This time we made it a block before he asked me to pull the car over so he could check something else. He went to the rear of the car and looked in one of his bags, returned to the car, and after apologizing for the inconvenience, asked me to please drive him back home. When I did, he returned to the car with another item. Although we then left his house for good, all the way to the airport Les checked and rechecked his pockets to make sure he had everything he needed. A simple trip to the airport had become an ordeal.

But the question remains: was Les mentally ill, or was his forgetfulness due to something else? Although I'm not a psychiatrist, I feel confident that it was something else. People who are mentally ill don't act like Les. If mental illness were making him forgetful and detached, it would have been because a tiny voice inside his head was telling him of all sorts of terrible things, and over time he would have become suspicious, angry, resentful, and in the end seek relief in drugs and alcohol. And that wasn't Les.

What I think Les had is adult attention deficit disorder, the mature version of the attention deficit disorder that—with or without hyperactivity—affects so many school-aged children. There is a popular series of books written by Drs. Hallowell and Raty whose titles share the words "Driven to Distraction" and that explain how attention deficit disorder prevents both children and adults from being able to focus their attention, making them appear forgetful. Unfortunately for Les, until recently attention deficit disorder was thought to be a problem that affected only children and then disappeared before adulthood, making it nearly impossible for adults to receive treatment. But times have changed, and no one believes that now.

CHAPTER 10: ROMANCE

3. June 20, 1980—Bob and Caroline's Wedding at the Home of Les and Cheryl Naman

In February of 1980, I attended that year's Recent Advances in Neurology meeting in San Francisco. This was an annual event and one of neurology's best meetings, with San Francisco's dining and entertainment as additional attractions. In past years I had gone alone, meeting up with my friends Dr. Roger Curran and his wife, Anne, from Nampa, Idaho, but due to the recent change in my romantic status, this year Caroline would be going with me.

Caroline and I were now madly in love, and since lovers are always on the lookout for romantic opportunities, we had decided to combine the meeting in San Francisco with a car trip along the California coast to the Hotel del Coronado across the bay from San Diego. So, after the final lecture, Caroline and I said goodbye to the Currans, rented a car, and began driving south along California Highway 1, a spectacular stretch of road that hugs the coast from San Francisco to San Diego.

Although the two cities were only five hundred miles apart, a distance that could be driven in a day if you wanted to push it, we were in no hurry to get anywhere soon. In fact, we had three days before we were expected at the Hotel del Coronado.

Northern California's winter weather is, like Portland's, overcast and wet, but after passing through Monterey, the skies cleared and the rest of our trip was in Southern California sunshine.

Highway 1 features some of the most magnificent sights, quaintest towns, and most enchanting scenery in the world. After leaving San Francisco, the highway passes the surfing and beach boardwalk community of Santa Cruz, the cities of Monterey and Carmel, the wine-growing country of San Luis Obispo County, the Hearst Castle, the Spanish architecture of Santa Barbara, the Santa Ynez wine country, LA's Huntington Beach, and finally, San Diego itself. February and March are also the months that the gray whales and their calves migrate from Mexico to Alaska along the Pacific coast and are visible from the highway.

To add to the trip's diversity, 1980 was the year of the thirteenth Winter Olympics, hosted by the United States and taking place in Lake Placid, New York. The games ran from February 13 to February 24, but we had been so busy in San Francisco that we were only peripherally aware of their existence. But now that our time was flexible, watching the games quickly became one of our favorite nighttime activities.

While we were on the road to San Diego, we'd see the sights during the day, then rent a motel room, slip into bed, and watch the Olympics at night. Due to their use of performance-enhancing drugs, the Soviets and East Germans would eventually take forty-five medals to our meager twelve, but there was still plenty of drama to keep us entertained.

On the third day after leaving San Francisco, we pulled into the Hotel del Coronado. The hotel had been given rave reviews by several of our friends, but it still exceeded our expectations.

Nicknamed "the Del," the Hotel Del Coronado was a historic beachfront hotel occupying a spit of land between San Diego Bay and the Pacific Ocean. When it opened in 1888, it was the largest resort hotel in the world. Although it no longer holds that honor, it is still—after the Tillamook Air Museum in Tillamook, Oregon—the second largest wooden structure in the world, and one of the few remaining examples of the wooden Victorian beach resort. It was also one of the first hotels to be lit with electric lights, the wiring personally overseen by Thomas Edison.

Visually, the Del is an architectural fantasy. From the outside, it is a huge, sprawling, hodgepodge of shapes in white and red. White, shingled walls lined with windows, porches, and decks alternate with a seemingly random assortment of red roofs—both flat and conical—dotted with dormer windows and capped with turrets and brick chimneys.

Inside, the Del's lobbies, bars, libraries, dining rooms, and ballrooms are immense, with huge, ornate chandeliers hanging from the ceilings. Its walls and ceilings are covered with rich, polished wood fashioned into bold and intricate designs.

When I made the reservation, the only amenity that I requested was that our room face the ocean. That room turned out to be *two* spacious rooms, a bedroom and a sitting room, more comfortable than luxurious and painted in cool whites and grays. The outside walls were lined with high windows opening onto a spacious deck, and beyond that were the beach and ocean. And yes, at the foot of the bed there was a large TV for watching the Olympics.

We left our rooms only once. Toward the end of our stay we drove to San Diego Harbor, rented a small sailboat, and sailed around the bay for a couple of hours. I think we did this more to confirm that we were still capable of existing outside the Del than from of any desire to sail. But other than that one excursion, we stayed in our suite, ordered our meals from room service, and whenever we weren't otherwise occupied, watched the Olympics. We checked out of the Hotel del Coronado the day after the "Miracle on Ice" victory by the American hockey team over the mighty Soviets. It's hard to imagine how a vacation could have been any better.

The Engagement

We flew back to Portland and resumed our lives, but after California, I knew that Caroline was who I wanted to spend the rest of my life with, and I couldn't stop thinking about proposing to her. So one quiet, rainy Sunday afternoon, I asked if she would marry me, and she said yes. Although I had never talked to her parents, I called their home in Mexico, Missouri, and asked her father, Jack, for permission to marry his daughter, and he gave us his blessing.

THE LOVEHANDLES

Caroline wanted an outdoor wedding in June, and the Namans had generously offered us the use of their home. Built on a steep hillside overlooking the city, the view from the Namans' home was spectacular. The wedding would be in their backyard, which was reached by descending a long flight of stairs from the deck off their kitchen. Dinner and dancing would follow. Although it was a wonderful time for Caroline and I, it was a sad time for the Namans, who after two children and many years of marriage, had decided to call it quits.

I had met Les a few weeks before and liked him immediately. Like Bart, Tom, Ed Kuehnel, and George Sample, Les did his residency at OHSU and had worked as an internist for Kaiser Permanente ever since. Les was also a piano player, and because he wasn't tolerating the divorce as well as his wife, Cheryl had suggested that Les might find some comfort being in the band. We had happily given Les a tryout, and to our mutual good fortune, he was now officially a member of the Lovehandles.

Caroline was planning the wedding, with Cheryl as her principal consultant. My only responsibilities were to ask Larry Franks to be my best man and arrange for the band to play after dinner.

When I told Larry that Caroline and I were getting married and asked if he would be my best man, Larry was at first delighted. But then he became thoughtful and said that before saying yes, he would need to know the extent of his duties, just to be sure that the job of best man wasn't too demanding. I asked him for an example of something that would be too demanding, and he said that given how busy he was, having to travel to each of the seven continents to gather stool specimens to bring to the wedding was probably more than he could do. I said that as far as I knew, no stool specimens would be needed, and he had only to wear a suit, seat Caroline's mother before the ceremony, and stand with me while Caroline and I exchanged vows. Reassured, he agreed to be my best man.

Next I asked the band if they would play at the party. They said they would, but then they wanted to know how that would work if I couldn't play the drums. I'd been taking drum lessons and said that I would ask my drum teacher if he would be willing to sit in for me; and when I did, he was happy to do so. And with that, my wedding preparations were over.

But for Caroline and the Namans, the work had just begun. Although I'm sure that it was happy work for Caroline and Cheryl, I remember seeing poor Les planting fresh flowers in the flower beds up until the day of the wedding. Preparing for our marriage as his own was falling apart must have been very hard on him.

The guest list was about fifty people, with several of Caroline's relatives flying out from Missouri, the Currans driving from Idaho, and my old friends Larry Armstrong and Alan Houser coming from Kansas and Minnesota.

Mount Saint Helens

You may recall from the list of my Portland homes that house number four was on the northern flank of Mount Tabor, an inactive volcano within Portland's city limits, and had an unobstructed view of Mount Saint Helens, an active volcano only fifty miles north of Portland in Washington State. Remember? Good. Well, Mount Saint Helens was about to be very, very naughty.

On March 20, 1980, Mount Saint Helens experienced a magnitude 4.2 earthquake, and one week later, its north face began bulging and venting steam. In response, the local TV and radio stations began running nearly continuous updates of Mount Saint Helens's frequent seismic activity, as well as issuing increasingly frantic warnings aimed at clearing the mountain of all workers, residents, and visitors before it blew.

But while that was going on, Caroline and I were in a very different world, our minds more on each other and our wedding than anything geologic. More precisely, in the week beginning Sunday, May 11, 1980, we were trying to decide which member of the clergy would perform our ceremony and had made plans to evaluate the pastor of the Congregational Church the following Sunday.

THE LOVEHANDLES

Since the service we'd be attending didn't begin until 11:00 a.m., we lounged in bed as long as we could before getting dressed. Around 10:30 a.m., we walked out Caroline's front door to find an inch of gray volcanic ash covering everything. Unknown to us, at 8:32 a.m. that morning a second earthquake—magnitude 5.1—had triggered the collapse of the mountain's north face, setting off the deadliest and most economically destructive volcanic event in U.S. history. For the next nine hours, plumes of ash shot into the sky, spreading ash as far east as Boise, Idaho; as far north as Edmonton in Alberta, Canada; and, of course, liberally over Seattle and Portland.

But undeterred, we brushed the ash off my car and drove to the Congregational Church, where the minister passed muster and agreed to perform our ceremony.

Our Soundtrack

Like many courtships, ours had its own musical accompaniment. 1979 and 1980 were wonderful years for music, and when we were at Caroline's house, the stereo was always playing. We began our relationship listening to everyone that was popular at the time—Donna Summer, the Bee Gees, the Knack, ABBA, Bad Company, the Police, Fleetwood Mac, Robert Palmer, Pink Floyd, Anne Murray, the Village People, Blondie, Queen, the Talking Heads, Prince, Dire Straits, the Pretenders, Steely Dan, and Bruce Springsteen—but as our feelings for one another crystalized, so did our musical preferences, until we were listening exclusively to two artists whose lives were separated by nearly three hundred years: Johann Pachelbel and Bob Seger.

Around 1680, German baroque composer Johann Pachelbel wrote what has come to be known as Pachelbel's Canon in D. Although this piece was popular during Pachelbel's lifetime, it soon went out of style and was virtually forgotten until 1919, when it was republished by musical scholar Gustav Beckmann.

Also slow in coming was the first recording of the Canon, which was in 1940 by Arthur Fiedler and the Boston Pops Orchestra. Although Fiedler's recording was lush and sensuous, the tempo was much sprightlier than the slower, dreamier versions we are used to hearing today, and their recording attracted little attention. The critical change in tempo came in 1968, when the piece was recorded by the Jean-François Paillard Chamber Orchestra. Still, it was not until 1970 that a San Francisco radio station playing Paillard's recording was unexpectedly inundated with listener requests for more, and suddenly, after nearly three hundred years, the Canon was back in business. Since then, Pachelbel's work has been recorded by numerous artists on numerous labels and has become one of the most popular classical pieces of all time. Paillard's recording was featured on the soundtrack of Robert Redford's 1980 film *Ordinary People*, which won four Academy Awards, including Best Picture. But nowhere was Pachelbel's Canon in D appreciated more than it was in Caroline's house on 1927 SW Edgewood Drive.

At the other end of the continuum was Bob Seger and the Silver Bullet Band, who between 1976 and 1980 recorded three classic albums: *Night Moves, Stranger in Town*, and *Against the Wind*. Those three albums contained such gems as "Night Moves," "Mainstreet," "The Fire Down Below," Hollywood Nights," "Still the Same," "Old Time Rock and Roll," "Feel Like a Number," "We've Got Tonight," "You'll Accompany Me," "Her Strut," "Against the Wind," and "Fire Lake," which expressed every nuance of emotion that Pachelbel's Canon missed. In the days before our wedding, those four records—the three by Seger and Pachelbel's Canon in D—were in exclusive and constant rotation on Caroline's turntable.

The Wedding

On the afternoon of Friday, June 20, 1980, I entered the Namans' house, passed through the kitchen where children in their party clothes were getting final instructions from their parents, and walked out onto the deck. Caroline's two boys, Tim and Bill, were both there, wearing tuxedos and looking very sharp. A string quartet of young women from a local college was playing on one side of the deck, while a bartender was serving wine on the other. I descended the stairs to the lower level, where several rows of white chairs faced the line of trees at the back of the yard. A few of the guests were already seated, and the rest were standing in small groups, talking and sipping their wine. I saw my best man standing in one of the groups and joined him.

When the string quartet began playing Pachelbel's Canon in D, it was the signal for the program to begin. I disappeared around the side of the house to await my entrance, and Larry left to find Caroline's mother, the lovely white-haired lady who everyone called "Marnie." Once Larry had seated Marnie, I walked down the aisle and took my place beside him, turning to watch as Caroline's dad brought my beautiful bride-to-be down the aisle to my side. Although I was later told that my legs were visibly quivering during our vows, the ceremony went on as planned, and we were pronounced man and wife.

After the wedding, the party moved upstairs to the house, where the string quartet played, drinks and dinner were served, toasts were made, and the cake was cut.

Then the Lovehandles, who had set up in the children's playroom next to the kitchen, began playing. First Caroline and I danced, then Caroline danced with her dad and I danced with her mom. Shortly after that, Caroline's parents excused themselves and left for their motel, and we were alone with our friends.

The Namans' house hung on a steep hillside beside a narrow, winding street, and because parking would have been a problem, we had hired a couple of high school kids to serve as valets. David Black, Caroline's brother-in-law from her previous marriage, had given us a grocery sack full of marijuana as a wedding present, and once Marnie, Jack, and the couples with kids had left, the valets began rolling joints for the partygoers.

It was the most wonderful night of my life. About 2:00 or 3:00 a.m., as the party was winding down and the remaining guests had collapsed in the living room, Larry Franks began expounding on the topics of turgor and sheen. At first this seemed utterly nonsensical, especially in the context of a wedding, but in Larry's hands it became a remarkable display of intellect, imagination, and humor.

Defined scientifically, "turgor" is the firmness of tissues due to their degree of hydration. For example, the skin of someone who is well hydrated has a palpable tautness that is lacking in the skin of someone who is dehydrated. "Sheen," on the other hand, is a characterization of an object's reflectivity to light and may be expressed in terms of luster, patina, gloss, brilliance, radiance, brightness, or any number of other similar qualities. Although both of these subjects could have been presented so blandly as to be snooze-worthy, Larry's dissertation gave them a depth of meaning and nuance that made them fascinating. As filtered through Larry's mind, turgor and sheen became in turn foreboding, whimsical, confounding, frightening, and finally hilarious. How he did that, I'm not sure.

Does this make any sense? Probably not. I think you had to have been there.

CHAPTER 11: AFTER THE WEDDING

4. September 17, 1980—Kathy's Mother's Birthday Dance
5. July 18, 1981—Dental Hygiene Association's Outdoor Concert
6. December 6, 1981—Angel's House Party
7. Date Unknown—Bowman's Resort (with Carlos on the Bass)

Following the band's successes at the Samples' New Year's party and our wedding, we had a couple of performances that were considerably less successful. In fact, they failed miserably. However, they were important in terms of our musical education.

The band's first gig after our wedding was a birthday party dance for a nurse's mother held in a huge room that had formerly been either a synagogue or a Greek Orthodox Church. Although the first set began well enough, after a few songs the sound just disappeared. Never having experienced this before, we blithely continued playing in the hope that the sound would somehow fix itself, but after several of the guests complained, we stopped playing while Tom and Bart puzzled through a temporary fix of the problem.

We resumed playing, but after a few more songs the problem recurred, and this time Tom Hoggard's guitar amplifier stopped working entirely, most likely because of a blown fuse. Since Tom's guitar and both vocal microphones—Patti's and Tom's—were being fed through Tom's guitar amplifier, our only option was to route everything—both vocal mics, Tom's guitar, Les's keyboard, and Bart's bass guitar—through the bass guitar amplifier and hope that it didn't blow too. Fortunately it didn't. Although we eventually made it through our program, the sound was faint and murky, our performances were shaky, and the party was irreparably damaged. It was all very embarrassing.

THE LOVEHANDLES

But once we were back in Tom's basement and Tom and Bart had replaced the fuse, our sound system seemed to be working again. As it would turn out, we were missing the real cause of the problem, but at that time we were too naïve to understand its true nature.

The following summer we were asked to play a concert for the Dental Hygiene Association in a public park. Although the weather was beautiful and there was a nice bandstand for us to play from, there were no electrical outlets on the bandstand. But after some investigation, outlets were found in a building behind the bandstand, and by connecting several extension cords end to end to bridge the distance between the outlets and the bandstand, we seemed ready to play.

But even with everything connected, powered on, and at maximum levels, we were generating sound at levels no higher than a whispered conversation. At first we thought it was a recurrence of our previous problem—the blown fuse—but our sound engineers-in-training, Bart and Tom, went through everything and were unable find a problem. We were putting out sound, but very faintly. At first this puzzled us, but eventually we understood that playing outside required a much greater volume of sound than playing inside, where the sound was confined and free to reverberate between the various surfaces.

But knowing that didn't help us once we were outside in the middle of a performance. There were people who had come to the park expecting to hear a band, and either we had to issue an apology, pack up our stuff, and leave, or we had to stick it out and play our full program at inadequate levels. We chose the latter and went song by song through another cringe-worthy performance, though this one was made slightly less embarrassing when a number of people stayed to hear what they could of us.

Music and Electronics

When did popular music become so dependent on electronics? The process began in the late 1940s and early 1950s when big band music

106

was fading and rock and roll was coming into prominence.

Big bands first became popular in the 1920s and reigned supreme for almost three decades. Their fall from grace was the result of several factors. The first was that big band music went out of style. Although the big bands of the 1920s, 1930s, and 1940s played short, catchy, dance-oriented music, the jazz orchestras that replaced them—the Duke Ellington and Stan Kenton Orchestras, for example—played longer, more complex compositions that were designed for listening rather than dancing. And once people stopped dancing to big band music, it ceased being popular.

Factors two and three were logistics and money. The amount of planning that went into a single big band performance—multiplied several times for an entire tour—was huge, and the price of feeding, housing, transporting, and paying fifteen or more musicians (plus the band's support team) became prohibitive.

And the final factor was technology. With electronic amplification, a four- or five-member rock band could play venues far larger than the big bands and generate much more money in the process. It was therefore no coincidence that the death of the big band era and the birth of rock and roll coincided with the development of the electric guitar and amplifier.

The usual sound system for a band like ours began when the output cords from the vocal microphones and the electric instruments—guitar, bass guitar, and keyboards—were plugged into a flat, rectangular piece of equipment called a mixing board. Mixing boards had eight or more parallel rows, or "channels," of identical knobs and sliders that were moved to adjust the tone and volume of each input to produce a listenable "mix" of sound for the entire band. Next, the output from the mixing board was relayed to a powerful electronic amplifier, which increased the signal many times and sent it on to two separate sets of speakers. The first set of speakers—the "PA," or public address system speakers—were larger and faced the audience, while a second, smaller set of speakers—the "monitor" speakers—sat on the stage floor and faced the band. Monitor speakers enabled the members of the band to hear each other, which was critical, since the electric instruments themselves produced very little sound by themselves.

In contrast to such a system, our sound system was laughably primitive and, as we discovered, totally inadequate for certain situations. Instead of having a separate mixing board, amplifier, and speakers for the band and audience, Tom's guitar amplifier and Bart's bass guitar amplifier were our whole sound system. Although these units had their own tone and volume controls, amplifiers, speakers, and input jacks, they were small. A typical guitar amplifier was only about two feet high, two-and-a-half feet wide, and a foot deep, while a bass amplifier was somewhat larger. These amplifiers were designed to allow the guitar player and the bass player to hear themselves, and that was it. They were not designed to supply sound to the rest of the band or to the audience. Although our system worked well enough in small spaces like the Samples' dining room or the Namans' playroom, in larger spaces, where the volume had to be turned to maximum levels, either fuses blew or the sound was inadequate.

The last two gigs had taught us the importance of a powerful and flexible sound system, and although none of us knew anything about sound systems, it was clear that we needed one. Because I had developed a friendly relationship with John Chaissang at Showcase Music and Sound, I was given the job of learning about sound systems. This turned out to be surprisingly difficult, and I took several trips to Showcase before I understood how sound systems worked—and in turn, how much we could expect to spend if we bought one.

Finally, I presented my findings to the band and was given permission to buy an inexpensive sound system. I returned to Showcase and bought four Peavey speakers—two large floor speakers for the audience and two smaller, wedge-shaped speakers for the band, as well as a PX 200 Dual-Powered Mixer, a single piece of equipment that combined an eight-channel stereo mixing board with two one-hundred-watt amplifiers.

In time we outgrew the PX 200 and bought a five-hundred-watt-per-channel Crown amplifier, a sixteen-channel Peavey mixing board, bigger speakers, and something called a "snake," which was a 150-foot cable that allowed us to connect up to sixteen inputs to a mixing board situated at the back of the hall and was operated by a sound technician.

Band Practice

Wednesday nights came to be associated with band practice like Sundays were with church. Although band practice was occasionally canceled because of a conflicting event—an illness, an important meeting, or the birth of a child—that was rare, and the words, "Sorry, can't do it, we (or they) have band practice that night," were recited by band members, spouses, friends, secretaries, and office managers whenever Wednesday nights were proposed for other activities.

For many years, band practice was held in the basement of Hoggard's house, which was located in the quiet suburban neighborhood of Sylvan. But because our playing was loud enough to be heard throughout the neighborhood, it became a sort of community event. That no one complained about the noise was a testament to Hoggard's standing in the community and the tolerance of his neighbors.

Band practice began promptly at 7:00 p.m. I was in charge of bringing the alcohol, which was usually a half-gallon of Gallo Hearty Burgundy purchased at a local convenience store. Our arrival was followed by a brief period of conversation, and then we got down to business, which usually began with a presentation and discussion of any job offers that had been received the preceding week. Because of their larger social networks, gigs usually came through Hoggard or Patti and Bart.

One of the problems with being a band of doctors was "call." Call was a block of time—usually 24 hours or more—when a doctor had to be available to answer questions from patients and doctors by phone or if needed, care for patients in the hospital. This meant that if the band were offered a gig when one of us was on call, unless that doctor could trade his call with another doctor, we couldn't accept the job. And since there were four of us in the band who took call, sometimes we had to refuse jobs.

But early in our musical career, as long as we were all available, we accepted any gig that came along. That didn't last long. As we learned more about the differences between audiences and discovered our own limitations, we became more selective about what we accepted.

At practices, after we had finished discussing new job offers, we went over the status of upcoming shows. Since Patti and Bart usually handled our bookings, they would be the ones to pass along any new information about scheduled performances—such as when to be there, what to wear, or how to get into the building.

This was followed by reports from band members who had been given the tasks of investigating the cost or availability of any ancillary equipment (like stage lighting, strobe lights, mirror balls, or fog machines) or personnel (such as sound or light technicians) that were needed for a particular gig.

But if there were no upcoming gigs to prepare for, then new music would be introduced for the band's consideration. A new song could come from any member of the band; its presentation typically accompanied by sheet music and/or copies of the song's lyrics, plus a recording of the song for the band to hear. Listening to the song was followed by a discussion of its merits and weaknesses and estimates of how well we thought we could play it. If the overall reaction was favorable, we might try playing it a time or two before filing it away for future consideration.

But if we had an upcoming performance, which was most of the time, we spent the rest of the evening going through the set list, playing the songs that needed work and omitting those that didn't. We usually finished around 11:00 p.m.

A Joyous Noise?

Ever since the Lovehandles began playing publicly, there's been a question that I've never been able to answer. That question is, "Why did people like us?" Although we had our moments, the Lovehandles were not a very good band. Our singer could be flat, the drummer seldom maintained a steady beat, and the saxophone and keyboard players rarely made it through their solos without obvious errors. We lacked the musicianship to duplicate the identifying riffs of the songs we played, at best playing no more than approximations of their key musical phrases. Even on our best nights, we never played a song from start to finish without errors. And yet people liked us. Why?

But before tackling this question, I need to confess that not everyone liked us. Although it would be accurate to say that most of the people who hired us were satisfied with what they got, there were a few who weren't.

Early in our musical career, when we were anxious to play for whoever would have us, we sometimes took jobs that in retrospect we shouldn't have taken. I remember one gig that we had been told was to be a "house party" but turned out to be something very different. What we got instead of the wild, inebriated, dance orgy that we were expecting was a small group of people who just wanted to get together, sip some wine, talk, and have some unobtrusive but competently rendered music playing softly in the background—which I suppose could be defined as a "house party," even though it wasn't our definition. Although such a party would have been ideal for many musical groups—string quartets and jazz combos for example—it was wrong for us. First of all, we were incapable of playing anything softly; it was either loud or louder. Second, we didn't play well enough to be the kind of band you just sat and listened to.

When we arrived for this supposed house party, we were met by a handful of young people and directed to the basement, where we were told to set up in the corner facing a few tables surrounded by chairs. When we were ready to play and the chairs had filled up with guests who were more interested in talking than dancing, we knew we were in trouble. Although we did our best to please them, their eyes, expressions, and body language told a different story. Early on Patti tried to change the party's direction and get them to dance, but when they wouldn't budge from their chairs, she wisely backed off. It was a very uncomfortable night for everyone, but the experience helped us define our limitations. After that we were careful to vet job offers by asking how many guests were expected, would alcohol be served, and was it to be a dance party.

But if you didn't judge us musically, there were many things about us to like:

1. We were dependable. If we took a job, we arrived on time and left when we were told to leave.

2. We were cheap. As professional people by day, we didn't need to make much money from our music—just enough to cover expenses and preserve our self-respect. If we happened to be paid well for a performance, it was more often because we had been offered the money up front than because we had asked for it. But even then, I can't recall ever making enough money from a single gig to bother paying ourselves. Whatever was left over after expenses went into an account for future purchases.

3. We were flexible. We adapted our performances to fit the occasion. Whatever the reason for the party—whether it was a house party, an office party, a divorce party, a birthday party, a wedding, an anniversary, or a bat mitzvah—we chose music that was appropriate for the occasion. If the party was honoring a particular person, a couple, or a group, then we learned their ages, backgrounds, and musical preferences and tried to play their favorite music.

4. We were clean, courteous, and friendly. We were unlikely to look or smell bad, get in fights, steal things, or leave a mess.

5. We were unusual. Although today there are enough doctor bands in Portland that contests between them have become an annual event, in our day we were a rarity, and hiring us was a novelty.

6. Like Johnny Limbo and the Lugnuts, we worked hard to show people a good time. We may have been musically

challenged, but we tried to look and sound our very best. We hired technicians to do our sound and lights; we rented disco balls and smoke machines; we had dance competitions—disco contests, limbo contests, and twist contests—and gave out prizes; we even wore costumes.

7. But most of all, people liked us because we were fun. There was nothing elitist or stuffy about the Lovehandles. We were a party band, plain and simple, and if you were willing to drink, dance, and overlook a few musical mistakes, chances were excellent that you would have a good time.

Dance

Defined as a series of movements matched to the speed and rhythm of a piece of music, dance has been around since the beginning of civilization. It has been used to depict a society's history, to accompany its ceremonies, and in times of need, to summon rain, a bountiful harvest, or victory in war. On an individual level, dance has been used to demonstrate endurance, physical prowess, and sexual attractiveness. In modern times, it is most often a means of courting and a pleasurable form of social interaction.

The only groups that restrict dancing seem to be religious, which either forbid it on certain religious holidays or, fearing that dancing may release dangerous sexual impulses, forbid it altogether. But viewed generally, most societies have either condoned or encouraged dance. And from its near-universal place in human history, somewhere within our DNA there exists a desire to dance.

Why do we dance? In simplest terms, we dance because it makes us feel good. Scientific studies have shown that the combination of music and dance triggers the release of four feel-good neurotransmitters— serotonin, dopamine, endorphins, and oxytocin—which individually and collectively act within the brain to make us feel happy.

113

THE LOVEHANDLES

Anatomy of a Party

I'll set the scene of a party we might have played. The musicians have assembled their equipment, tuned their instruments, completed their sound check, and are ready to play. Across the dance floor, the partygoers have had a few drinks and are waiting for the music to begin. Let the good times roll? Not necessarily. Just because a group of people and a band come together at the same time and place, there is no guarantee that the two will click—none whatsoever.

For a group of skilled and seasoned musicians, this situation produces little or no anxiety. They've been in this position many times and have a very good idea of what to expect. They know that in all probability, the party will be a success; the crowd will love them, and in no time at all everyone will be out on the floor dancing their butts off. But then again, maybe not. As I said, nothing is guaranteed, and if—God forbid—the worst were to happen and no one danced and everyone left the party early, will these musicians be crushed? Well, of course they'll be disappointed, but they won't be crushed. The reason is that these musicians have the luxury of both talent and experience, and they will know that it wasn't their fault. After all, they played well enough. They always do. No, the problem was the audience, who was either too tired or too disinterested to make it a party. But sometimes that happens, and there's no reason to feel bad about it. Next time will be better. C'est la vie.

But let's say that instead of skilled and seasoned musicians, the band is composed of four doctors and a dental hygienist who are relatively new to the music business and more than a little bit insecure about their musicianship. What are they thinking at such a party?

First of all, they are hoping that the crowd isn't expecting musical perfection, because if they are, they'll be disappointed. Then, after studying the crowd, they may be surprised to see a somewhat different demographic than they had envisioned—perhaps the people are a little older or a little younger than they were expecting—and now they're wondering if they've chosen the right music. Will it fit the occasion, will the audience like it, and most of all, will they dance to it? Because if they won't dance, it's going to be a long night for everyone concerned, and it will be the band's fault.

Meanwhile, on the other side of room, members of the audience are having their own concerns. Perhaps they're a little overweight—as most people are—or maybe their clothes are less flattering or fashionable than they might wish. Or they learned their dance steps a few decades ago and haven't changed them since. Or there are a number of people in the audience that they don't know and who may be critical of their dancing. Or maybe their boss is there, or someone they are secretly hoping to impress. And what if the band plays a bunch of Latin numbers that they don't know how to dance to? The synthesis of all their concerns is, simply, "Will I be embarrassed if I get up and dance?"

The truth is that every party has an initial inertia, a resistance that must be overcome before people are willing to get out on the dance floor and risk making fools of themselves. And audiences vary. Some groups are less self-conscious and some are moreso, and at the beginning of any party, the band never knows exactly what it's going to get.

The Great Facilitator

Although we called ourselves the Lovehandles, to most people we were Patti and the Lovehandles. And when the party was over, the guests may not remember the Lovehandles, but they remembered Patti, who was both the band's face and its heart.

The word "moxie" is defined as "the ability to face difficulty with spirit and courage," "force of character, determination, or nerve," or "courage, spunk, or attitude," and there was no one in the band with more moxie than Patti Dunahugh. And had it not been for her fearlessness and determination, the Lovehandles would most likely have drifted into oblivion after the Samples' New Year's Eve party.

But Patti would not allow that to happen. She was driven to perform, and long after the Lovehandles had gone their separate ways, Patti continued to entertain her friends, sometimes composing elaborate theater pieces for their holiday get-togethers. It was simply who she was, and in the context of the Lovehandles, entertaining meant getting people on their feet and out onto the dance floor, feeling the music and getting caught up in the moment.

This sometimes was no mean feat. Not only did it take courage to stand before a group of strangers and dare to entertain them, but doing so with the Lovehandles providing the music didn't make her job any easier. Yet night after night Patti was up to the challenge, willing audiences to dance and have a good time.

But Patti didn't do this blindly. She knew that when people came to a dance, they wanted to dance. Although they might act like dancing was the furthest thing from their minds, Patti knew otherwise. There was something in people that made them want to get up and move in time to the music, and because dancing would make them feel good, she knew that if she could get everyone up on their feet and moving, the party would be a success.

But the "get everyone up and moving" part was where the challenge lay. Although people wanted to dance and felt good once they did, there were risks associated with the act.

Foremost, perhaps, was the risk of rejection. Although this was less likely to be a factor in social situations where partners, either through dating or marriage, had been previously established, even established partners may have no interest in dancing, at that particular moment or ever. So rejection was still a possibility.

But even after a couple had agreed to dance, dancing still had its unknowns. For at that point, instead of simply talking or watching other people dance, a couple needed to demonstrate a knowledge of dance steps, a sense of rhythm, and a modicum of athletic ability. And because dance carried certain sexual connotations, dancers should either look good or at least think they do.

Obviously, there's a lot at stake when a couple takes the dance floor. So what will make it easier for them? There's alcohol, which should be available and easily accessible. But alcohol alone won't help everyone. Although it will grease the skids for many, others will need further assistance. So how do you convince this group that the benefits of dancing outweigh its risks? You bring in Patti.

Patti Dunahugh was the most powerful weapon against dance party inertia ever devised. First of all, Patti was not someone you ignored or refused. She was a powerful presence, persuasive and relentless, and if Patti wanted you to dance, chances were good that you were going to dance. But at the same time Patti was clever, and unless you were paying close attention, you might not understand that she was persuading you to dance.

The music usually began with Neil Diamond's "Sweet Caroline"; a song familiar to all, loved by most, and easy to dance to. Patti would watch to see who got up to dance and who held back. Two more danceable numbers would follow. Often people didn't need much encouragement, but if no one was dancing by the fourth song, she might mention that all the party needed was one courageous couple to break the ice. "After all," she might joke, "the band has spent hours preparing for tonight, and you wouldn't want all that practice to go to waste, now would you?" It was friendly and funny, but she had made her point: she expected the audience to dance.

Then after another song or two, a few people might move out onto the dance floor, but if the number of dancers was still not enough to satisfy Patti, she might remind the audience that the reason we were all there, both band and audience, was to have a good time. "Isn't that right?" she might ask. "And here," she would say, pointing to the dance floor, "is where the good times begin. Besides," she might add, "isn't dancing good for you? Doesn't it make you smile, and isn't smiling good for you? Of course it is! Everyone knows that. And I'm not even talking about all the exercise you'll get dancing. So, come on people, let's get healthy!"

As the evening wore on and more members of the audience were separated from their inhibitions and drawn to the dance floor, Patti would begin working on the few remaining holdouts. She might suggest that they didn't have to dance; they could just get up and move. "Of course," she would say, "moving isn't dancing, but it's just as good for you, isn't it? And if you don't have a partner, you can dance by yourself, or pair up with another single, or join a couple and become a threesome. And girls can dance with girls, and boys can dance with boys. It really doesn't matter, does it? After all, we're all friends here, aren't we?"

And with that, a surprising number of the non-dancers, single or otherwise, would finally get up and join in the fun. Really, it was a joy to see.

Angel's Gig

In the ten years that the Lovehandles were in existence, one gig stands out as my favorite. On December 6, 1981 we played a party at the home of Angel Pilatto, a young woman that our recently divorced piano player, Les, was dating. Angel was an administrator at one of the local hospitals, and on the night of the party her home was filled to bursting with a lively mixture of friends and coworkers who were anxious to have a good time. You could feel it in the air.

Angel was a character, a bit on the loud side, maybe a little bossy, but friendly, outgoing, and a natural hostess. Her house was small, cozy, and decorated for Christmas, the lights turned down to create a sense of intimacy.

We set up in the dining room, and with the first bars of "Sweet Caroline," the guests began dancing—and they never stopped. They responded to us, and in turn we fed off their enthusiasm. Not only was there interplay between band and audience, but there was also a newfound communication between the band members, an awareness of what each of us was playing that made the music come alive. My own playing had never been better. It was as though I had somehow broken free of my self-consciousness and become a real rock-and-roll drummer.

Interspersed in any song are short drum patterns called "fills," which occur at the end of a musical phrase and serve to conclude that section and introduce the next. Though drum fills seldom last longer than a measure (four beats of a 4/4 song) they allow the drummer considerable creative license, and if executed properly will add to a song's interest and musicality. Not knowing that drum fills had a name, Hoggard called them my "dum-de-dums," and at one point during the night Tom leaned over and said that he was loving my dum-de-dums.

Patti guided our play, and instead of stopping when we came to the end of the first set, Patti called out another title and off we went. We tackled stuff that we may have played only once or twice before—or sometimes not at all—but everything we played, we played well. It was just one of those nights when the conditions were perfect and the music happened.

The guests filled the entire first floor of Angel's home, dancing shoulder to shoulder and hip to hip. We played until they could no longer dance, and they danced until we could no longer play.

The night wasn't just great fun; it also taught us that our potential was much greater than what we had previously suspected, and that under the proper circumstances we were a pretty good band.

That night I'd recorded the party on a small cassette tape player, and after that, whenever I wanted to hear what we could be, I would take it out and listen. The recording wasn't perfect—there was a lot of background noise, and our playing wasn't as good as it had seemed at the time—but all things considered, it wasn't too bad. As mistake-ridden as our playing could sometimes be, there was something wonderful there. And though we had many good nights after that, I've always felt that Angel's party held a magic that we were never quite able to duplicate. It was, to me, as close to perfection as we ever came.

THE LOVEHANDLES

Set List For Angel's Party,
December 6th, 1981

Set One

1. "Sweet Caroline," by Neil Diamond
2. "Mr. Bojangles," by Jerry Jeff Walker
3. "July, You're a Woman," by John Stewart
4. "Cotton Jenny," by Gordon Lightfoot
5. "Nothing but a Heartache," by Wayne Bickerton and Tony Waddington, as sung by Bonnie Tyler
6. "Summer Wine," by Lee Hazlewood
7. "Love Potion No. 9," written by Jerry Leiber and Mike Stoller and performed by The Clovers, The Searchers, and The Coasters
8. "You Are So Beautiful," written by Billy Preston and Bruce Fisher as performed by Joe Cocker
9. "The Tide is High," by John Holt as performed by Blondie
10. "Proud Mary," by John Fogarty and Creedence Clearwater Revival

Added: There were several but "House of the Rising Sun," as sung by Eric Burdon and the Animals is the only one I can remember.

Set Two

11. "Somebody's Knockin'," by Jerry Gillespie and Ed Penney, as sung by Terri Gibbs
12. "Bette Davis Eyes," by Donna Weiss and Jackie DeShannon, as sung by Kim Carnes
13. "Run Around Sue," by Dion
14. "Blue Bayou," written by Roy Orbison and Joe Melson, as sung by Linda Ronstadt
15. "Queen of Hearts," by Hank DeVito, as sung by Juice Newton

120

16. "Cobwebs and Dust," by Gordon Lightfoot
17. "Yellow River," by Jeff Christie
18. "Hot Stuff," written and sung by Donna Summer
19. "Say Good Bye," I'm not sure who wrote this
20. Medley: "Hit the Road, Jack," Percy Mayfield, as sung by Ray Charles; "Louie, Louie," by Richard Berry, as performed by The Kingsmen; "What'd I Say," by Ray Charles; and "Twist and Shout," by Phil Medley and Bert Berns, as sung by The Isley Brothers

All vocals were by Patti.

Bowman's

We followed Angel's gig with a party at Bowman's, a resort on the western slopes of Mount Hood. Although Bart had been playing bass on most of our songs, he was really a saxophonist, and Tom had just learned that his new next-door neighbor, Carlos, was a bassist who had played with Buddy Holly—or so Carlos claimed. Tom invited him over and Carlos practiced with us a few nights, and when we asked if he would play with us at Bowman's, he said he would.

But despite the supposed distinction of playing with Buddy Holly, Carlos was a mystery. I eventually even came to doubt the Buddy Holly connection. Although Carlos may have been the world's greatest bass player, he played so softly that it was impossible for me to tell if he was really a Buddy Holly-caliber bassist or not. And when, in a friendly effort to get to know him better, we asked Carlos about his past, we got no clear answers. All that we knew about him was that he owned and operated a tiny Mexican restaurant in the food court of Portland's Yamhill Market, he had an attractive wife and a new baby, and he lived next door to Hoggard in a very nice home. Beyond that, Carlos was an enigma. And in part because this was around the time of *The Godfather* films, Hoggard concluded that Carlos was living in Portland courtesy of the witness protection program.

The Lovehandles

Bowman's would be the nicest venue we had played to date—a definite step up—and we were anxious to play well. In contrast to the house parties that we had been playing, Bowman's had a stage and a dance floor, and we would be uncharacteristically dressing in coats and ties for the occasion.

Before the party we were to meet on stage, set up our equipment, and do a sound check. But when everyone showed up for the sound check except Carlos, we searched the building and found him in the restaurant, having a leisurely dinner with his wife. Although we tried to coax him away from his dinner for the sound check, Carlos just continued eating.

Carlos *did* show up for the dance, where he continued to play so softly I couldn't hear him. Although the party went well enough, Carlos seemed disinterested in being "one of the guys," and after the sound check incident, we weren't particularly interested in having him in the band either, so we didn't ask him back. And if Carlos was anything besides a bass-playing restaurateur from Texas, we never found out.

Dreams

Unless you're Sir Richard Branson, Jeff Bezos, Elon Musk, or some other obscenely rich person, you've undoubtedly dreamed of a life that is better than the one you're living. In fact, dreaming of a life more glamorous than your own is practically inescapable. For example, turning on your car radio and hearing that the lottery has a jackpot of nearly half a billion dollars instantly triggers a vision of what your life would be like if you won it: how you'd quit your job, pay off your debts, give a bundle of money to charity, and sell your house—it wouldn't matter if you got a good price or not—then buy a big fancy place in town, and maybe something ultra-modern with lots of glass at the beach, too. Both homes, naturally, would come with swimming pools, maids, and furnishings selected by some famous decorator. In addition, you'd drive only the coolest cars, maybe a red Tesla convertible for around town and some big tricked-out, self-driving SUV for road trips. Then you'd hire your own dietician and lose all that weight you've always wanted to lose, or better yet, you'd get one of those operations that does it for you; then you'd spend a lot of time in the gym with your personal trainer until you looked awesome; and then you'd walk into some cutting edge clothing store and buy a bunch of exciting new clothes—whatever struck your fancy.

But suddenly you realize that the odds of winning that half-billion-dollar lottery are so infinitesimally small that it's not even worth wasting your money on a lottery ticket, and POOF! Your wonderful fantasy is swept away by the much grimmer reality of your real life. But it was fun while it lasted.

One of the most appealing aspects of being in a band is just how easily a band lends itself to fantasizing, but on a much more satisfying level than simply imagining that you won the lottery. Instead of being the dumb schmuck who got lucky and won that jackpot, you can now dream of your band making a hit record, or maybe a whole series of hit records; of having your picture on the cover of *Time* and *Rolling Stone*; of making more money than you know what to do with; and of having beautiful women—or men—wanting to sleep with you. And although you can still have the same big houses, cool cars, great body, and amazing clothes that you would get if you had won the lottery, this time, instead of being lucky, you *earned* it. You earned it because you were talented. You, my friend, were a creative artist. And you did it all on your own—well, maybe there was a little luck involved—but you did it *mostly* on your own. And the key to turning those dreams into reality is making a hit record.

I'm sure that there wasn't a single one of us who didn't occasionally dream of making a hit record and living the rock-and-roll fantasy life, but the rest of the time no one thought that recording an album was a good idea—except Hoggard.

For example, if we played a successful gig and people came up to us afterward and complimented us, saying that they enjoyed our music and they had had a great time, and asked where we were playing next, at the very next practice Tom would remind us how well the party had gone, how many compliments we got, and suggest that we make a record.

Sure, it's always nice to hear someone imply that you're good enough to make a record, but I can't remember anyone in the band ever saying, "Yes, Tom, that's a great idea! Let's go make a record."

First of all, studio time is very expensive, and then you have to play your song until it's mistake-free—and knowing the Lovehandles as we all did, that could take years. And second, nothing that we played was original. Every song had been someone else's hit, and by the time it had gotten around to us, there was no meat left on the bone.

Besides that, I'd recorded almost all of our performances, first on tape and later on a small digital recorder, and I knew exactly what we sounded like. I had even taken some of our better recordings to the hospital and played them for the nurses, technicians, and doctors, and though everyone was unfailingly polite, never once did anyone say, "Hey, you guys should make a record."

So beyond recording the parties that we played, the Lovehandles never recorded. And I still think that was a very good decision.

Top: Scott Huff (center) with son, Jamie, and dad, Charlie, in 1987.
Bottom left: Picture taken by Bob's sister, Nancy, of Leo, Louise, Bob and Mugsy. *Bottom right*: Nancy Crumpacker with her high school prom date.

THE LOVEHANDLES

Top Left: Tom Hoggard (guitar) *Top Right:* Patti Dunahugh (singing)
Bottom: Bob Crumpacker (drums)

 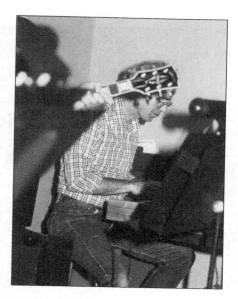

Top Left: Bart McMullan *Top Right:* Les Naman
Bottom: Psychiatrist, friend, drummer, sound man,
and videographer, Warner Swarner

The Lovehandles in 1986.

Top Row:

Tom Hoggard, Les Naman, Bart McMullan, Bob Crumpacker

Bottom Row:

Patti Dunahugh and Mike Bragg

Top: Marie and Ed Kuenel

Bottom: Marie Kuehnel, George Sample, and Caroline

Top: Bob, George, and Tom Hoggard

Bottom: Bob, George, and Larry Franks

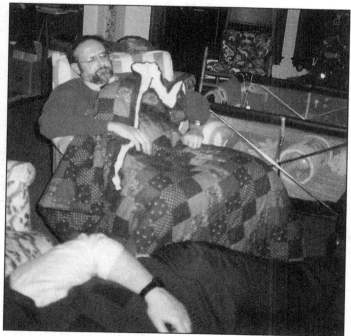

Top: Mike Bragg, Dr. Mary Burry, and Patti

Bottom: Bob (foreground) and Tom Hoggard sleeping it off

Top: Bill and Tim after our wedding (1980)
Center: Bill, Tim, and Andy, Christmas (1988)
Bottom: Andy (2014)

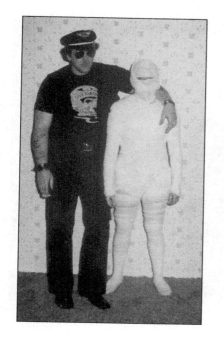

Top Left: Biker and mummy (Bob and Caroline)
Top Right: Cheryl Naman (Woods) on tambourine

Bottom Left: Cheryl and Les (1975)
Bottom Right: Patti sailing (1988)

Top Left: Larry and Urike Franks fishing on their honeymoon (1985)
Top Right: Mike and Patty Bragg (2018)

Bob and Caroline Crumpacker (2005)

CHAPTER 12: MIKE

8. September 12, 1982—Edgewood Road Block Party

During the fall of 1982 we were asked to play a block party on Edgewood Road, which you may recall was the site of Caroline's home before we got married. After the wedding, Caroline and I had made the surprisingly difficult decision to sell her home and move into mine, and when some of her old Edgewood Road friends heard that I played in a band, in order to see Caroline again they had asked us to play.

We were joined in our practices leading up to the block party by Mike Bragg, a statistician and computer expert who was working for a local medical review organization. Bart and Patti had met Mike at a party in the home of Dr. Robert Manley, an Adventist Medical Center orthopedist, where Mike was singing and playing the guitar. Bart and Patti had been so impressed with him, both personally and musically, that they invited him to play with the band to see if we might be compatible. Although Mike did his best to fit into the band without calling attention to the discrepancy in our skill levels, he was clearly a member of that rare and intimidating breed of cat that we reverently referred to as "real musicians." But he was such a nice guy and seemed so eager to play with us that when we asked if he would like to join the band, he accepted. We could hardly believe our good fortune.

But beyond being impressed with Mike's personality and musicianship, I have no memory of the block party. I'm sure that Mike fit easily into the band, sharing vocals with Patti and playing rhythm guitar behind Hoggard's lead. And in response to Mike's playing, I'm also certain that we did whatever we could to raise the level of our musicianship—but unfortunately no actual memories of the party exist.

THE LOVEHANDLES

Mike Bragg

Mike Bragg was a very orderly person. Although he was big—six feet, one inch tall and over two hundred pounds—he never looked rumpled. He was always, as they say, nicely put together. Although he seldom wore anything but casual attire, it was always good stuff, coordinated and attractive. Likewise his grooming was impeccable: his thick, dark hair was always neatly trimmed, and a neatly trimmed moustache and/ or beard appeared or disappeared from his face at random intervals.

His mind, too, was well organized, and not just with the little day-to-day stuff. Mike had carefully considered life's big issues, and to the best of his ability he had formed opinions based on a rational evaluation of the facts. Although he was raised a Catholic, he had examined religion at an early age, and,when it made no sense to him, he became an atheist—case closed. Expressions like "free and easy," "spur of the moment," or "by the seat of your pants" did not apply to Mike Bragg.

Although he had rejected religion, Mike was a man of principals; his credo based on a fairness that was both inclusive and sympathetic. But recognizing that this was only his view of things, Mike never insisted that others think the same way. Within reason, you could do what you wanted, but Mike was going to do what he thought was right.

Unless he was performing, Mike was a private person, which made communication through music an attractive alternative to conversation. In social situations it was easier for Mike to interact with others— especially strangers—by performing for them than by conversing with them on any number of difficult and unpredictable topics Someone once told him that they knew more about him after listening to him sing than they did after talking to him—and that was probably true.

When Mike wasn't performing , he was often quiet, sometimes for extended periods. At these times his brow would crinkle and his expression would become pensive, as though he were involved in some difficult internal negotiation. But once he spoke, he did so thoughtfully, his voice warm and modulated, his words pertinent and meaningful. And if you had been waiting for his reply, it would have been worth the wait.

He was devoted to his family and helpful to his friends, and as far as I know, he had no enemies. This is his story.

In 1943, two years after America had entered World War II, a young man by the name of Don Bragg dropped out of high school and joined the Navy. Three years later he met his wife-to-be, Lucille Powers, at a USO dance in San Pedro, California. They married in 1948, and on March 9, 1949, the first of their four children, Michael Eugene Bragg, was born.

After leaving the Navy, Don earned his GED and moved to Torrance, California, where he began working on the assembly line of the Douglas Aircraft Company. But finding little opportunity for advancement, he decided to take his chances with Douglas's competitor, the Northrop Corporation. Although Don had little formal education, he had learned some electronics in the Navy and impressed his new bosses with his intelligence and drive. He advanced rapidly, ultimately earning the title of test flight engineer.

Don's wife, Lucille, was born in San Antonio, Texas, but her family moved frequently during the depression, finally settling in San Pedro, California. Partially located in San Pedro, the Port of Los Angeles was a major international seaport that served a number of important functions for the U.S. Navy during World War II, not least of which was hosting the USO dance where Don and Lucille first met.

In 1958, Don was transferred from Northrop's plant in Torrance to their aircraft test center at Edwards Air Force Base near Mojave, California, where he designed electronic equipment to monitor and record the flight data of experimental aircraft. At Edwards, Don worked with Chuck Yeager and other test pilots of the "Right Stuff" era, along with astronauts from the Mercury and Gemini space programs.

Although Don worked at Edwards, the family lived in Lancaster, a desert community of twenty thousand about twenty-six miles south of Mojave, the region home to cactuses, desert tortoises, jackrabbits, rattlesnakes, tumbleweeds, and the sonic booms of experimental aircraft.

Mike describes his father as a typical 1950s man who saw himself as the family breadwinner and little else. In fact, everything that Mike learned about what his father thought of him came from his mother in statements like, "Your father was so proud of you!"

But Mr. Bragg was not completely absent from his son's life. As a Boy Scout leader, he led Mike's troop on a number of arduous hikes; more significantly, though, he took an active interest in Mike's choir performances. During his concerts, Mike would often look out into the audience and be surprised to see his father sitting there. Although Mr. Bragg never praised Mike directly, in later years he would ask Mike to sing and play the guitar for him, then listen with what Mike interpreted as a mixture of pleasure and pride.

Although Mike knew that his mother had sung in her high school choir, she was very shy about singing around the house, and only rarely did Mike catch her singing to songs on the radio. But there was nothing shy about Mike's maternal grandfather, William Powers. Mr. Powers worked as a shipwright in the San Pedro shipyard, but when he wasn't working, he was an Irish tenor who sang at weddings, funerals, and the christenings of new ships.

He visited the Braggs frequently, singing songs such as "Animal Fair" and "Hinky Dinky Parlez-Vous" to the children. But he also loved the music of Stephen Foster, and one of his favorite songs was Foster's "Hard Times." After listening to his grandfather sing the song many times, Mike came to love it, too. In fact, years later Mike recorded it with his daughter Lori, and during the Great Recession, Portland's public broadcasting station did a series of shows under the title of "Hard Times" about how local people were coping with the recession. Looking for different versions of the Stephen Foster song to play during the programs, the station asked for submissions, and when Mike and Lori's version was the first to be selected, Mike appeared on the show to explain his relationship to the song.

When Mike was nine years old and in the fourth grade, his father was transferred from Torrance to Northrop's test flight facility near Mojave, California. Although it was hard for Mike to leave his old school, his new school in nearby Lancaster had something that would make the move worthwhile: a choir.

One day while his class was singing, a woman entered the room and began walking up and down the aisles, pausing to listen to each child sing. After listening to Mike, she tapped him on the shoulder and whispered that he was to meet her in the cafeteria after class.

Although Mike had no idea what the tap had meant, he went to the cafeteria anxious to find out. There the woman explained that she was the director of the school choir, and the tap meant that she would like to have him in the choir. Mike was ecstatic. Singing was important in his family, and he was delighted to hear that he, too, might be a singer. Until then, all he had ever heard about his singing was that on hot days in Torrance he would sit outside under the lawn sprinkler singing "Singing in the Rain" at the top of his lungs—a story that his mother told to make people laugh.

At Lancaster's Antelope Valley High School, Mike not only sang in the school choir but also with a group from the choir called the Balladeers, with a folk trio named Three's a Crowd, and with three football players in a barbershop quartet. The singer-guitarist for the Balladeers was a boy by the name of Jeff Cotton, who went on to play lead guitar in a rock group called Captain Beefheart and the Magic Band. Beefheart, whose real name was Don Van Vliet, was a Lancaster native whose music achieved critical acclaim and cult status during the 1960s and 1970s. The Magic Band's album *Trout Mask Replica* was ranked fifty-eighth on *Rolling Stone's* list of the five hundred greatest albums of all time. Although Mike never met the Captain, Van Vliet's father drove a delivery truck for a local bakery and was well known to the Braggs.

In high school, Mike tried to get his parents to buy him a guitar, but fearing that a guitar might lead him astray, his parents refused. If he wanted a guitar, they said, he would have to buy it himself.

THE LOVEHANDLES

So Mike spent thirteen dollars of his own money on a guitar from Sears, Roebuck, and Company. The guitar came with a book of chords and a recording of notes to tune the guitar with. At first, the guitar's steel strings made Mike's fingers bleed, but he kept playing, and eventually his fingers toughened up.

After Mike had learned a few chords, he formed a band called the Fortays—the imaginary plural of the word "forte," a musical term meaning to play loudly. Mike's band played the music of the Byrds, Bob Dylan, and Simon and Garfunkel, while their high school rivals, a band by the name of the Jungle Jive Five, played the harder rock of the Rolling Stones, the Doors, and the Who. When the two bands faced off in a battle of the bands, the Jungle Jive Five won. Mike conceded that they had been the better band.

During the summer between his freshman and sophomore years of high school, Mike and Dana Coleman, the drummer of the Fortays, were walking down the street when a convertible sped by full of girls waving and yelling at them. The girls continued circling the block until Mike and Dana agreed to ride with them. One of the girls was Patty Ann Gribbin, who Mike would date throughout high school, fall in love with, and eventually marry. When asked how he and Patty met, Mike always answers, "She picked me up."

After high school Mike stayed in Lancaster to attend Antelope Valley Junior College. During his first year at the junior college, Mike's band continued to play, but they broke up after two of its members were drafted into the Army. After that Mike got some jobs singing at weddings and parties, but little else.

Following junior college, Mike and Patty married and moved to San Bernardino, where Mike attended the University of California, Riverside. Although he had initially enrolled in a pre-med curriculum, Mike became fascinated with the science of behavior and the mind, and he switched his major to psychology with an emphasis on research.

Mike had a number of work-study jobs in the animal labs at Riverside, but of all the studies he was involved with, his favorite concerned the song of the white-crowned sparrow. The professor conducting the study and the reason for Mike's interest in psychology was Dr. Ivan Petrinovich from Moscow—Idaho. Standing less than five feet tall, Dr. Petrinovich was not only a clever researcher but also a stand-up bassist in a local avant-garde jazz band, which Mike saw as an intriguing combination.

The professor had noticed that the song of white-crowned sparrows was different in different areas, and he wanted to find out whether these regional differences were inherited or learned—the old "nature versus nurture" question.

For the study, Dr. Petrinovich first identified trees containing nests of white-crowned sparrows by listening to the birds' songs with a long, bazooka-like instrument that focused sound. He then climbed the trees to gather their eggs, then took the eggs to his laboratory and separated them into three nests—each in its own soundproof box. And finally, he piped different sounds into each of the three boxes. In the first box, the baby sparrows heard nothing but white noise; in the second box, they heard the song of the white-crowned sparrow; and in the third box, they heard the song of the Oregon junco, a bird related to the white-crowned sparrow but with a different song.

A complication of the professor's research occurred when a policeman saw a man wielding a bazooka-like device climbing trees, and detained him for questioning. And when the officer learned that the suspect was Russian, it did nothing to lessen his suspicion. But finally Dr. Petrinovich convinced the officer that his behavior was part of a research project, and no charges were filed.

When the white-crowned sparrow eggs hatched, Mike's job was to feed the baby birds. He would dip a stick into a gruel made of ground-up worms and poke it into the birds' mouths, being careful to do this quietly so that the sounds piped into the boxes would be their only auditory influence.

The song of the white-crowned sparrow normally consisted of a single high note followed by a number of trills and a long descending glissando (a glide from one register to another), ending on a single note in a lower register followed again by several trills.

THE LOVEHANDLES

The regional differences in the white-crowned sparrows' songs consisted of variations in the trills; the high notes, glissandos, and low notes were all the same regardless of where the birds were from.

The study showed that the birds exposed to the white noise sang the same high note, low note, and glissando as did white-crowned sparrows anywhere, but they omitted the trills; the birds exposed to the song of a white-crowned sparrow copied its song perfectly; and the birds exposed to the song of the Oregon junco sang the same high note, low note, and glissando as the white-crowned sparrow, but their trills were those of the Oregon junco. In other words, the birds inherited the same high notes, low notes, and glissandos, but they learned the trills from their environments—a combination of nature and nurture.

At Riverside, Mike sang in the university choir, which was much more demanding than any of his previous choirs. Getting a spot in the choir required the applicant to pass a rigorous audition. The music was difficult—Handel's *Messiah*, for example—and the practices were long. But Mike loved it. He also sang in taverns and at parties, and in a few school skits.

Mike graduated from Riverside in 1972 with a bachelor of arts. His next academic goal was to get a master's degree in psychology, and for that he and Patty moved to Chico, California, where Mike attended California State University, Chico—also known as Chico State. Once again, Mike was focused on psychology research, but because the research required a statistical analysis of his findings, he was forced to learn statistics. Eventually he became a student advisor in statistics, helping PhD candidates with the statistical work on their dissertations.

Another interest born of necessity was computer science. Although personal computers would not be available for another decade, much of Mike's statistical work required computer analysis. Computers were very different in the 1970s than they are today. Computers then were massive machines that were housed in their own air-conditioned buildings. The data that they analyzed was entered on punch cards at sites called terminals, which connected to the mainframe with hefty electrical cables. Although he didn't know it then, his knowledge of statistics and his facility with computers would become two of his most valuable assets.

Mike also got the opportunity at Chico State to perform regularly. He had a steady gig singing and playing the guitar for the psychology department's Friday afternoon keggers, and he performed at a number of local bars and taverns.

He also sang on radio commercials. Although he usually did this as part of a duo or group, he once sang a commercial for the Wood Brothers' Carpet Company by himself. At one of the weekly psychology department get-togethers, he sang the Wood Brothers jingle, and a professor laughingly told him, "So that was you! I can't stand that commercial, and now I know who to blame."

When Mike and Patty were invited to parties, Mike was usually asked to bring his guitar. At one party, Jery—with one "r"—Graves, a young man Mike had sung with on several commercials, brought his stand-up bass, and after a brief rehearsal in the back bedroom, they performed together. They were a big hit, and after that they were frequently asked to play at functions, always to appreciative audiences. At the peak of their popularity, Mike and Jeri appeared on a local TV country music show called *The Moriss Taylor Show*. Although they had never played much country music, they learned a few songs by Buck Owens and Hank Williams, and their TV debut was a success.

Then after earning a master's degree in psychology, it was time for Mike to find a job, but there was a problem: although his studies had focused on research, actually performing research required a PhD. The only thing that his master's degree qualified him to do was sell insurance.

But Mike had an idea. If he stayed at Chico State for another year and did some additional coursework, he could become a certified school counselor, and that seemed like a worthwhile goal. But while Mike was pursuing counseling, he learned that with a little more coursework he could become a school psychometrist, which was a psychologist who performed and interpreted psychological tests—intelligence tests, personality tests, and vocational aptitude tests—and that sounded even better than counseling.

THE LOVEHANDLES

But after completing all the coursework, Mike discovered that certification in psychometry also required an internship, and that was bad news. First, internships took six months to complete; second, he had just completed an internship in counseling; and third, internships were unpaid. And that was the deal-breaker. By then Mike had been going to college for seven years, he had accumulated considerable student debt, and he and Patty had two children. Mike could not afford to go another six months without an income. So when Mike was offered a job as a school counselor in nearby Paradise, California, he took it.

Mike worked at Paradise High School for six months, then began working four hours in the evening advising students who were working toward their GEDs and four hours in the morning managing a sheltered workshop for adults with mental disabilities. The work was enjoyable, and the split schedule gave him a chance to be with his children during the day, but then California voters passed Proposition 13, a property tax limitation bill that dramatically reduced the state's income. This hit the public schools hard, and the school district where Mike was working wanted to cut his job down to half-time. But Mike and his family could no more survive on half his salary than they could on nothing, so he began looking for work elsewhere.

He found a job at the Superior California Professional Standards Review Organization (SCPSRO), reviewing the hospital stays of Medicare patients with respect to the necessity of their admissions, the length of their hospital stays, and the efficiency of their discharge planning. In recent years, the cost of medical care had skyrocketed; because of this, Medicare was looking for ways to save money, and had created professional standards review organizations (PSROs) to make this happen. Mike's particular job involved tracking statistics to see if their organization had been effective in reducing the number of hospital admissions and the length of their stays, and then comparing their results with those of other PSROs throughout the country. Although he had taken the job not knowing what to expect, he found the work fascinating.

MIKE

The job had nothing to do with his background in psychology. He had qualified because of his knowledge of statistics, skill with computers, and familiarity with hospitals. You see, in addition to his education and the jobs that I have already mentioned, Mike had also been working at hospitals. While he was in junior college, he had worked at the Antelope Valley Hospital as an emergency room technician, a job similar to that of a high-level orderly. At Riverside Community Hospital he held a similar job, and after he and Patty had moved to Chico, Mike had worked at Feather River Hospital. These jobs had given him a good understanding of how hospitals worked.

Although he always assumed that one day he would return to counseling, the pay at the SCPSRO was so much better than what he'd been making as a counselor that he stayed at the job for three years.

Then there was a shake-up among the California PSROs. When Mike first began working for the SCPSRO, there were twenty-eight review organizations in California, but it had finally dawned on Medicare that twenty-eight PSROs was far too many, and they pared the number down to just two—one for northern California and one for southern California—and when that happened Mike was suddenly out of a job.

Now Mike was at a crossroads. Should he look for another PSRO job or return to counseling? Although counseling was important, the work he had been doing at the SCPSRO seemed important, too. Since he had been there, Mike and his coworkers had developed a number of methods for measuring medical outcomes in new, more scientific ways—and they were saving Medicare money.

For example, whenever someone hit their head, it was common for them to go to an emergency room to get checked by a doctor, who would then order a series of skull x-rays looking for a skull fracture. But after gathering all the data, the review organization found that unless there had been some initial sign of brain injury—loss of consciousness, dizziness, seizures, weakness, or numbness—the skull x-rays were invariably normal, and therefore unnecessary.

Then the emergency room doctors expressed concern that unless they ordered skull x-rays, they might be sued for not being thorough enough. But once again, the PSROs gathered the data and determined that in the absence of brain injury, no doctor had ever been sued for not ordering skull x-rays. So skull x-rays could safely be eliminated from many emergency room evaluations of head trauma—a significant cost-saving measure.

Not only were PSROs gathering important information, but the work was creative, exciting, and groundbreaking, so Mike decided to look for another PSRO job elsewhere.

Although there were no jobs in California, Oregon had two PSROs: the Oregon Foundation for Medical Care and the Multnomah Foundation for Medical Care, both based in Portland. Mike applied to the latter organization and was hired, and in 1980 the Braggs moved to Portland.

Five years later, there was a change in the structure of Oregon's PSROs as well. Medicare had decided that Oregon needed only one PSRO and merged the two organizations. The resulting organization was called the Oregon Medical Professional Review Organization (OMPRO). Although this was another opportunity for Medicare to eliminate unnecessary employees, by then Mike was a recognized leader in the field of medical cost analysis, and was asked to stay.

In the fall of 1982, Mike's wife, Patty, had been hired to do discharge planning at Portland Adventist Medical Center, and soon after that Mike and Patty were invited to a party at the home of Dr. Robert Manley, a Portland Adventist orthopedist. Mike had brought his guitar, and after playing a few songs he was introduced to Bart and Patti, who invited him to drop by Hoggard's some Wednesday night to play with the band. He did, enjoyed it, and agreed to join the band—and at that point the band was complete.

Mike's account of his life up until that point left me with a question: as an aerospace engineer, his father must have made a reasonable income; did his parents help pay for his education? Without any hint of anger or regret, Mike said no, he had never received any money from his parents. He and Patty had paid for his education, and as far as he knew, none of his siblings had received any money from their parents

146

for their educations either. In fact, he could not recall the subject of tuition or education costs ever being discussed in their home.

His sister, Diane, didn't go to college until she was in the workforce, and then her employer paid for her schooling. Though his father had gotten his brother Steve an entry-level job at Northrop, Steve made his own way and had done well. Shortly after being hired, he became interested in the plant's heating and lighting and had learned all that he could about it on his own. When computers became available, Steve used them to manage the plant's heating and lighting needs more efficiently. Mike's youngest brother, Jerry, had gotten a two-year associate's degree in supply line logistics, and at each of the three companies where he worked, he had come up with innovative solutions for difficult logistical problems.

These stories reminded me of Mike's father, Don, who had joined Northrop with no more than a GED and the electronics training he had gotten in the Navy, but who, through his own initiative, had worked his way up the employment ladder to become a test flight engineer. Perhaps he had created a template that his children had used to achieve their own successes—namely, "Use what you have and make your own way."

CHAPTER 13: THE NEARLY
FORGOTTEN YEARS—1982-1984

9. May 4, 1982—Angel's II
10. December 1982—Samples' II
11. April 9, 1983—Party at the Oregon Yacht Club
12. May 8, 1983—Dinner Dance for the
     Oregon Academy of Family Practice
13. November 11, 1983—Chis Mobleis's Wedding
14. December 1983—Unknown
15. February 11, 1984—Unknown
16. June 8, 1984—Navy League Dance
     at the Masonic Hall
17. June 19, 1984—Wedding
18. September 1, 1984—Wedding
19. November 17, 1984—Fiftieth Birthday Party

As you can see from this list, 1982, 1983, and 1984 were busy, but largely forgotten years in the band's history. Although three of our eleven gigs involved weddings, I can attach a name—Chris Mobleis, who I didn't know—to only one of them. The fiftieth birthday party likewise remains nameless, and the next two parties—the first in December of 1983, and the next on February 11, 1984—lack any form of identification. And though playing for the Oregon Academy of Family Practice must have been our biggest and most important gig to date, I can remember nothing about it. So of the eleven parties on the list, only Angel's and the Samples' second parties, the Oregon Yacht Club party, and the Navy League Dance remain in my memory.

THE LOVEHANDLES

Angel's II

Although we had been hoping for the same magic at Angel's second party that had characterized her first, things had changed. While Les and Angel had been in a promising relationship at the time of the first party, now they were in the process of breaking up. I don't know if this explained the night's muted tone, but the feeling of promise that had helped fuel her first party was missing. Although we played two competent sets, the interplay between band and audience that had sparked some of our best music at Angel's I was gone and simply couldn't be revived.

Samples' II

For the Samples' second holiday party, the Lovehandles opened for another doctor band headed by infectious disease specialist Mark Loveless. Mark was an excellent singer and lead guitarist, and most of his band's musicians (including their chiropractor drummer) were very talented. Although they blew us away musically, people listened to them and danced to us. So I feel like we did okay.

Oregon Yacht Club

Portland is divided into four quadrants by Burnside Street, which runs east and west, and the Willamette River, which runs north and south and empties into the Columbia River.

South of downtown Portland there is a community of thirty houseboats anchored along the east bank of the Willamette River. Although the Oregon Yacht Club was incorporated in 1900 to promote proficiency in boating and navigation, over the years it evolved from a boating organization to a houseboat community.

In the midst of these houseboats was a larger houseboat that served as the community's clubhouse and could be rented for parties. It was a single-story wooden building—approximately 120 feet long by 80 feet wide with tables and chairs, a stage, a dance floor, and a bar. The Oregon Yacht Club was one of the more magical places we ever played, and though I have no memory of whom we played for that night, powered by the sheer joy and wonderment of performing on a houseboat, this party was one of our best.

Navy League Dance, Masonic Hall

The Portland Rose Festival is a weeklong event held every June. It is organized and hosted by the nonprofit Rose Festival Association and run by volunteers. The festival features three parades: the Grand Floral Parade, the Starlight Parade, and the Junior Parade. Of the three, the Grand Floral Parade is by far the largest, and is viewed each year by over half a million people, second only to the Tournament of Roses Parade for the distinction of being America's largest floral parade.

In addition to the parades, the festival includes the coronation of a queen chosen from a court of high school princesses, ski races on Mount Hood, dragon boat races on the Willamette River, fireworks, carnival rides, concerts, and an air show.

Coinciding with Rose Festival Week is Fleet Week, when ships from the U.S. Navy, the U.S. Coast Guard, the U.S. Army Corps of Engineers, and the Royal Canadian Navy dock along the seawall of Tom McCall Waterfront Park to be viewed by the public. The ships vary from year to year, but they often include cruisers and destroyers—and sometimes even submarines.

Another Rose Festival-Fleet Week event is a dance for the visiting sailors, sponsored by the Portland Council of the Navy League of the United States. In 1984, the Lovehandles had somehow landed the job of playing for the Navy League dance, which was being held downtown in the Masonic Hall. I'm not sure how, exactly, we had managed to swing this, but I think that Patti knew someone in the Navy League, though I couldn't swear to it.

No longer associated with the freemasons, the Masonic Hall had become a venue for concerts, plays, exhibitions, and dances. The building was huge, standing four stories high and covering a quarter of a city block.

On the afternoon of the dance we were to set up our instruments and do a sound check with the hall's sound technician. We had never used a sound technician before and were both uncertain of the process and uncomfortable with the idea that the dance we were about to play would be big enough to require one.

Adding to our discomfort was the fact that we would not be playing for our usual demographic: professional people of about our same age who knew that we weren't really musicians. This time we would be playing for young sailors and their dates, kids who most likely knew their music and would want to hear us play it.

On the day of the gig we parked beside the building and carried our equipment through a side door into the hall. The scale of the place was overwhelming. It was grand in the way that halls built around the turn of the last century were grand: spacious marble hallways; high, ornate ceilings; and cavernous rooms. We loaded our equipment onto a freight elevator, ascended a couple of floors, and rolled it out onto a stage that must have been a hundred feet wide and fifty feet deep. The hall itself was huge, with a towering ceiling, a huge balcony, and a dance floor so large that a small army could have set up camp there.

My anxiety level leapt from merely uncomfortable to flat-out terrified. This was the big time; we were in the sort of venue that professional orchestras used for concerts and cotillions, and I felt very out of place. But of course there was no going back—we had committed to playing the Navy League dance, and that was that.

Once we had assembled our meager array of instruments, amplifiers, and speakers, the hall's soundman came on stage and placed microphones around my drums and cymbals, plugged all the output cords from the

microphones and instruments into a big receptacle in the center of the stage, and left. Minutes later he reappeared in the balcony behind a huge mixing board and asked us one by one to sing into our mics or play our instruments until he had cleanly captured the sound of each. When he asked me to hit a drum or cymbal, I was keenly aware of being unable to respond with any sort of cool little lick that I imagined real drummers played during sound checks.

Then he asked us to play something together, and when we stumbled through Creedence Clearwater Revival's "Proud Mary," I was never more aware of our imperfections. Every note sounded off key and out of rhythm. When the soundman was done with us, we filed out of the building, promising to meet backstage before the gig. It felt like we had just scheduled our own execution.

To compound our discomfort, Dr. Warner B. Swarner, a psychiatrist at Adventist Medical Center as well as a drummer in his own band, was going to record the occasion on VHS tape and would be meeting us backstage before the gig to set up his cameras.

When the time for our performance finally arrived, we shuffled out onto the huge stage and delivered the stiffest, most self-conscious, least spontaneous set of our career. Fortunately, the occasion was poorly attended. We had played several songs before the first wave of sailors arrived, and of those who stayed, only a few had come with dates. And of those, only a few danced. From time to time I would glimpse young men standing in the doorways at the opposite end of the room, assessing the situation and turning away.

Several weeks later the band was at my house for band practice—Hoggard had recently sold his home and was looking for another—and after practice Hoggard suggested that we watch Warner's tapes. Warner had recorded the event on two ninety-minute VHS tapes, which he had given to me. But in an effort to wipe the experience from my mind, I had never watched them. And before that night, no one from the band had asked to see them either.

But the passage of time had brought some healing, and when I asked the band if we should watch them, the consensus was that we should.

THE LOVEHANDLES

Reluctantly I retrieved the tapes and plugged the first of them into the VCR player.

It was worse than I expected. When the recording began, we were already out on stage playing something that barely resembled music. I was seated in back behind my drums while the other Lovehandles were standing in a row in front of me, our faces deadpan and our bodies nearly motionless. Although we were producing sound, nothing in our expressions or body language conveyed the slightest hint of enthusiasm or joy. We looked like six deer playing for a hunter's convention. Even worse, our lifeless delivery continued past the first few songs all the way to the end of first set, when we filed off the stage like pallbearers leaving a gravesite.

As the screen went blank we sat there stunned.

"Jesus," Les whispered, "that was terrible."

The rest of us agreed.

The first tape was followed by a discussion of whether or not we should subject ourselves to the second. Opinions were divided. Although some thought we had endured enough, others thought we owed it to Warner to watch both tapes. Finally, we decided to watch the second tape. "Maybe this one will be better," said the always optimist Hoggard.

I changed tapes, and as the second set was slowly becoming a copy of the first, something unexpected happened. On the fourth or fifth song, Bart, who had been standing like a wax figure holding a saxophone at the left end of the front row, turned slowly and walked to the right end of the front row, where he assumed the same position.

Although we were nearly catatonic by that time, someone saw Bart's move and asked me to play it again, which I did. Then someone chuckled, and someone else giggled, and I kept replaying Bart's move until we were all on the floor laughing hysterically.

Finally, we had recovered enough for Hoggard to ask the obvious question: "Bart, why did you move?"

There was a lengthy pause while Bart thought this over, and then replied, "I don't know, Tom, I guess I just felt like moving," which produced another round of helpless laughter.

154

Finally, we just let the tape run and watched it to the end. Except for Bart's move, there were no surprises. But by then we were feeling much better about ourselves, and vowed that in the future we would put both movement and expression into our play, and if necessary, we would do our damnedest to pretend that we were having a good time. And with that, we disposed of the most painful night of our musical careers.

CHAPTER 14: ANDY

On February 19, 1985, our son, Andrew Robert Crumpacker, was born at Adventist Medical Center. Caroline wanted us to have a child together and had gone through surgery to reverse the tubal ligation that she had gotten after her second child. Her surgery went smoothly, and although she had no trouble getting pregnant, staying pregnant was another matter. The surgery was followed by repeated miscarriages and numerous trips to fertility experts. But by the summer of 1984, Caroline was solidly pregnant.

When an ultrasound revealed that we were having a boy, we decided to name him Andy. A few weeks before that we had been at one of her son Tim's soccer games, where another player on Tim's team—bigger and stronger than the other kids—had been earnestly chasing the ball up and down the field in a selfless but futile effort to help their team win. But in those few minutes, you just knew that this was the kind of kid that any coach would be happy to have on his team and any set of parents would be proud to call their son. The boy had bright red hair, and the cheers from the sidelines told us that his name was Andy. Although Caroline and I had watched the game in silence, afterwards we both said how impressed we had been by the boy's effort and demeanor, and if our child happened to be a boy, we would name him Andy.

Although Caroline and I were by far the oldest couple in her Lamaze class (Caroline was 42 and I was 44), she did everything she could in terms of vitamins, diet, and exercise to ensure that despite our ages, our Andy would be the healthiest kid ever.

But it was not to be. On his first day of life, our own little red-haired Andy began having seizures. Since a leading cause of neonatal seizures is meningitis, Andy needed a lumbar puncture (commonly known as a spinal tap), and when a pediatric neurologist couldn't be found, I did the tap myself. It was normal. Next, Andy needed a CT scan of his head, but because Adventist's CT scanner was down for repairs, I rode in the ambulance with Andy to another hospital with an operating scanner. The scan showed that compared to the rest of his brain, the middle third of the right half of Andy's brain was abnormal. Although its contour was exactly the same as the identical area on the left side of his brain, the color of the area was darker, as though it were made of a denser material than the rest of the brain. But for the time being, there was nothing more to do than treat his seizures. So we started him on the standard medication for neonatal seizures, phenobarbital, and made an appointment for Andy to see a pediatric neurologist.

But the phenobarbital made no difference in his seizures, which came about every twenty minutes and lasted twenty seconds, just as they had done before he started the medication. Although most types of epileptic seizures—grand mal, petite mal, akinetic, and complex partial—can be identified by their appearance, Andy's didn't fit into any of the standard categories. Although they involved his whole body, they weren't grand mal seizures because first, Andy didn't lose consciousness during the seizures, and second, his arms and legs didn't jerk simultaneously and rhythmically during the seizures. Instead he was awake during his seizures, his arms and legs moving through a peculiar series of unsynchronized movements. But despite their frequency, Andy seemed comfortable with his seizures, which had probably been part of his life long before he was born.

During the winter days that I took care of Andy, I would often build a fire in the fireplace and lay in front of it with my son, watching the sparks rising off the logs and imagining that the peculiar patch of tissue on the right side of his brain was similarly sending off sparks to ignite his seizures.

Although I can't recommend the experience of watching your child have a seizure every twenty minutes, it helped being a neurologist. After headaches, seizures were the second most common condition that neurologists encountered in their day-to-day practices. At least I understood what was going on and could discuss it intelligently with his neurologist. But after a few months of proceeding logically through the entire antiepileptic formulary, none of the medications made much difference in Andy's seizures.

With no one else to turn to, Andy's neurologist called the most respected neurology center in North America, the Montreal Neurological Institute, described Andy's case to the neurologist on call, and asked for his suggestions. Whether the neurologist wanted to think about the case overnight or take some time to discuss it with his colleagues, he asked if he could call us with his recommendations the following day. He called the next day and told us to keep Andy on the same medicine he was currently taking and that Andy's seizures would eventually "burn themselves out," which we took to mean that in time, the brain cells causing Andy's seizures would simply die from exhaustion. When we asked how long that process would take, the neurologist said between fifteen and twenty years.

That answer was unacceptable. Andy had several years of growing up to do, and the idea of the three of us waiting patiently for fifteen or twenty years for his seizures to extinguish themselves was a ridiculous notion. Besides, we had a good idea that that abnormal chunk of tissue on the right side of Andy's brain was somehow responsible for his seizures, and we thought that if it were excised from his brain, then his seizures would either stay the same, improve, or go away completely. It seemed unlikely that surgery could make him worse. But no matter what the potential result, surgery seemed like the next step. The one fortunate feature of Andy's problem was that the single most removable part of the human brain was that very area on the right side of Andy's brain where the abnormal tissue was. Although that area participated in a number of important neurologic functions, those same functions were duplicated on the other side of the brain, which meant that the abnormal section of brain could be removed without hurting Andy.

Larry Franks had been following Andy's case with interest and agreed with our reasoning. The first thing to be done in preparation for a surgeon removing as much of an abnormal area as possible was to biopsy that area to find out what we were dealing with. "Biopsy" simply means to cut out a small section of something and submit it to a pathologist for identification, and in this case, Larry was willing to do the biopsy himself.

Around this same time, I made a startling discovery. This thing that we had been calling "Andy," which seemed to be little more than a tissue culture grown for the purpose of having seizures, was in fact a real human being. What's more, he was equipped with a full complement of human emotions, including a wonderful sense of humor.

My moment of discovery occurred on an evening when Caroline and I were visiting my sister Nancy and her boyfriend Rick. Andy was lounging nearby in his baby carrier, having a seizure about every twenty minutes. Prior to leaving for home, I took Andy out to our car and strapped him into his car seat. After connecting the last buckle I looked down at him, and as our eyes met, a big, happy smile spread slowly across Andy's face—and he laughed. In that instant this tiny infant, who until then had been more of a patient than a son, became the child that I loved without reservation.

Larry's biopsy revealed that the abnormality in Andy's brain was a rare but benign tumor, and Larry recommended that the surgery to remove it be performed by his mentor, Dr. John Girvin, chairman of the Department of Neurosurgery at the University of Western Ontario in London, Ontario. We took Andy to Canada, where Dr. Girvin removed most of the tumor. The surgery went well, and Andy would be seizure-free and off of all medicines for the next three months.

CHAPTER 15:
GAINING TRACTION — 1985-1986

20. March 16, 1985—OMPRO Party
    at the Multnomah Athletic Club
21. March 30, 1985—University of Oregon
    Dental School Reunion
22. September 5, 1985—OMGMA Party at the
    Great Hall in Sunriver
23. January 25, 1986—Bat Mitzvah at Nendel's Inn
24, February 15, 1986—Valentine's Day Party
    at the Franks' House
25. May 3, 1986—Linda Ficere's Wedding
26. May 31, 1986—Debra Olson's Graduation Party
    at the Multnomah Athletic Club
27. November 21, 1986—Brim Association Party
    at the Oregon Yacht Club
28. September 20, 1986—Irvington Neighborhood
    Association Party at the Irvington Club
29. November 13, 1986—Second OMGMA Party
    at the Salishan Lodge
30. December 6, 1986—Dr. Chenoweth's Christmas Party

Early in 1985 we were asked to play the OMPRO party at the Multnomah Athletic Club (the MAC). Although Portland had several athletic clubs, this was the city's oldest and most prestigious athletic club, on a par with those of Seattle, New York, and San Francisco.

Of course Mike Bragg, who worked for OMPRO, was the reason we had gotten the gig, but playing at the MAC was still a plum, regardless of how we got there.

THE LOVEHANDLES

The room where we would be playing was large, and we decided to do everything that we could to make the party a success. Warner Swarner, who had filmed our disastrous performance at the Masonic Hall, volunteered to do our sound, but in a room of this size, he wanted to control the sound from the back of the room, rather than from the stage. To do this we would need something called a snake, a 150-foot bundle of electrical cords that connected the microphones and instruments on the stage to the mixing board. And even though a snake would be our most expensive single purchase to date—350 dollars—we bought one.

Thanks to Warner, the snake, the MAC, and an enthusiastic crowd, the OMPRO party was one of our best to date.

OMPRO Set List

Set One

1. "Rip It Up," by Little Richard (Mike)
2. "Gloria," not the G-L-O-R-I-A of Van Morrison but the disco hit of Laura Branigan (Patti)
3. "What's Forever For," 1982 country hit sung as sung by Michael Martin Murphey (Patti)
4. "When the Feeling Comes Around," pop/country song sung by Jennifer Warnes (Patti)
5. "He's a Heartache (Looking for a Place to Happen)," Janie Fricke's third number one song on the country charts (Patti)
6. "Please Be the One," written and performed by Karla Bonoff (Patti)
7. "Tulsa Time," the Academy of Country Music single of the year as sung by Don Williams (Mike)
8. "Stand by Your Man," the Tammy Wynette classic (Patti)
9. "Hi-Heel Sneakers," blues favorite written and recorded by Tommy Tucker in 1963 (Mike)
10. "Queen of Hearts," up-tempo country song written by

Hank DeVito and sung by Juice Newton (Patti)
11. "Rock Around the Clock," Bill Haley and the Comets' rock classic from 1955 (Mike)

Set Two

12. "Old Time Rock and Roll," by Bob Seger (Mike)
13. "Hot Stuff," Donna Summer's disco hit (Patti)
14. "Sad Eyes," written and sung by Robert John (Patti)
15. Dion Medley: "The Wanderer," "Dream Lover," and "Runaround Sue" (Mike)
16. "Islands in the Stream," sung by Dolly Parton and Kenny Rogers (Patti and Mike)
17. "Can't Help Falling in Love," Elvis Presley classic (Mike)
18. "Heartbreak Hotel," Elvis Presley (Mike)
19. "Jailhouse Rock," Elvis Presley (Mike)
20. "Will You Still Love Me Tomorrow," written by Goffin and King, and sung by the Shirelles, it was the first number one hit by a black all-girl group
21. Dance Contest: "Everyday" and "Oh Boy!," by Buddy Holly (Mike) and "The Twist," by Chubby Checker (Patti)
22. "Tell Me a Lie," country hit as sung by Janie Fricke (Patti)
23. "Proud Mary," by John Fogerty, as sung by Tina Turner (Patti)

Set Three

24. "Gimme Some Lovin'," The Spencer Davis Group (Mike)
25. "Love's Been a Little Bit Hard on Me," another Juice Newton tune (Patti)
26. "Always on My Mind," as sung by Willie Nelson (Mike)
27. "You're No Good"/"She's Not There," Linda Ronstadt/The Zombies (Patti/Mike)
28. "In the Midnight Hour," by Wilson Pickett (Mike)
29. "Wipe Out," instrumental by The Surfaris, drum solo by Bob

30. The Everly Brothers Medley: "All I Have to Do Is Dream," "Let It Be Me," and "(Till) I Kissed You" the Everly Brothers (Mike)
31. "Shop Around," Smokey Robinson and the Miracles (Patti)
32. "Good Lovin'," The Rascals (Mike)
33. "Right Time of the Night," written by Peter McCann and sung by Jennifer Warnes (Patti)
34. "You're Only Lonely," J.D. Souther's 1979 hit single (Mike)
35. Medley: "Hit the Road, Jack," Percy Mayfield, as sung by Ray Charles; "Louie, Louie," Richard Berry, as sung by The Kingsmen; "What'd I Say," Ray Charles; and "Twist and Shout," Phil Medley and Bert Berns, as sung by The Isley Brothers (Patti)

The Great Hall

Two weeks after the OMPRO party we played a dance for the University of Oregon Dental School's class reunion. Then we had a break until September, when we were to play a dance for the Oregon Medical Group Management Association (OMGMA), the Oregon branch of a nationwide organization for medical office managers.

In the ten years that I had been in practice, medicine had changed dramatically. Due to the astronomical increase in the cost of medical care and the simultaneous decrease in doctors' salaries, the business end of medicine was now rife with changes that attempted to save doctors money. One–and two–doctor offices were being replaced by larger and more efficient specialty and multispecialty clinics run by office managers and staffed with office workers who specialized in specific areas of the medical business such as scheduling, insurance, and collections.

When I first entered private practice, medical secretaries needed no more than high school educations, but due to the growing complexity of medical practices, office managers were often expected to have college degrees and Certified Medical Practice Executive certification.

GAINING TRACTION

The OMGMA party was to be held in Sunriver, a resort community in central Oregon about twenty miles south of the city of Bend. Specifically, the event would be at Sunriver's Great Hall, a venue that I knew of because Caroline and I owned a vacation home in Sunriver. Although the Great Hall was familiar, the weekend would prove to be full of surprises.

We arrived in Sunriver on the day of the party to discover that the Great Hall was much greater than we expected. None of us had ever been inside the Great Hall, and what we had been picturing was a much smaller, more intimate venue than what actually existed. What we got instead was a massive wooden structure built from dark logs and planks with a wraparound balcony hanging above the periphery of a basketball court-sized dance floor. Although the room was not as big as the one we had played in at the Masonic Hall, it wasn't far behind, and our hearts sank when we realized that the sound system we had brought would be inadequate.

With only a few hours before the dance, we found a music store in nearby Bend that rented sound equipment, and drove there. Bend was a town of about eighty thousand in the midst of a recreational paradise offering golf, tennis, skiing, fishing, horseback riding, camping, boating, hiking, rock climbing, and mountain climbing; in fact, almost any kind of outdoor activity you can imagine. But those activities were primarily for visitors. At its heart, Bend was a cattle town surrounded by some of the best grazing land in the state. And though we should not have been surprised, we were still a bit taken aback to see that the music store was run by a young man dressed in cowboy garb whose name was Billy Bob.

But Billy Bob was a music man through and through. He was familiar with the Great Hall and knew exactly what we would need to put on a quality show there. In addition to a beefed-up sound system, he suggested that we consider some stage lighting to make the room lighter and more festive. And just as we were about to ask if Billy Bob knew of any sound and light technicians who were free that evening, he said that he would be happy to run the sound and lights himself. We could have kissed him.

The Lovehandles

Thanks in part to Billy Bob's help, the Sunriver party was a huge success. The other factor in the party's success was the OMGMA crowd itself, which was one of the best we had ever played for. They were young and enthusiastic, and danced from the first song to the last. We loved playing for them, and probably because we were doctors working hard for their approval—instead of the other way around—the feeling was mutual. It was the beginning of a wonderful relationship.

The Bat Mitzvah

We kicked off 1986 by playing an afternoon party at Nendel's Inn, a popular family restaurant and motel just west of Portland in a town called Beaverton. The party was a celebration of the coming of age—the bat mitzvah—of a twelve-year-old Jewish girl. The better-known male counterpart of the bat mitzvah was the bar mitzvah. We had never played a party for either and learned a couple of new songs—"Hava Nagila" and "Sunrise Sunset"—appropriate to the occasion. It was a great honor to have been asked to play for this girl's celebration, and we did our best to make her day a memorable one.

Larry Franks Again

In 1977, Larry married a girl named Jonelle Williams. Jonelle worked in what was then known as the A/V (audio-visual) Department of the Adventist Medical Center. She was tall, attractive, and athletic, and she'd grown up in Eugene, the home of the University of Oregon.

Shortly after announcing their engagement, Larry asked me to be his best man, but a few days later he told me that Jonelle had requested that her brother, Kevin, be his best man instead. Without being too specific, he let me know that members of her family had *demanded* the change. But he promised that I would be invited to the rehearsal dinner the night before their wedding.

The rehearsal dinner was held in one of the darkest, least inviting taverns I had ever been in—which is saying something. A mural involving mountains, trees, and elk painted in Day-Glo colors adorned the wall behind our table. Although the dinner should have been a joyous occasion, a sense of discomfort hung in the air, and instead of my lively, happy friend who was so much fun to be around, Larry seemed tense and distracted.

After the waiters had brought our food, Larry suddenly bowed his head and asked us to join him in prayer. I was shocked. Never once in all the countless times that we had been together had Larry ever shown me his religious side. But Larry launched into a long, fervent, and multifaceted appeal to God to forgive his shortcomings, to bless their marriage, and to bless all the people both living and dead who were or had been important to their lives.

Much of my surprise came from not being a religious person myself and assuming that Larry wasn't either. My own lack of religion was probably due to the fact that even though my parents had dragged my sister and I to church once or twice a month, neither of my parents were particularly religious. In fact, my father once told me that while he thought that religion was a "force for good," he didn't believe that there was a God.

Of course, it could also be argued that more people have been killed in the name of religion than for any other reason, but despite the probable truth of that assertion, I tended to agree with my father: I thought that religion was still a good thing overall. I didn't think that the problem was religion itself. It seemed more likely that people just didn't need much of an excuse to kill each other, but after doing so they *did* need some noble-sounding reason to rationalize their actions, and of the available choices, religion seemed to be the most popular.

But despite my cynicism, from time to time I have felt that not being religious was a deficiency that I needed to correct. I've gone to different churches and read various religious works in an effort to kindle a spark of piety, but to no avail. For whatever reason, I am stuck being a skeptic.

167

The Lovehandles

Listening to Larry's prayer reminded me of a time in high school when I went with my friend Bill Hull to the Christmas Eve service at the local Episcopal Church. Bill and I were the starting tackles on our high school football team, and Bill was both a very nice kid and a very tough kid. But shortly after we entered the church, Bill dropped to one knee, bowed his head, and began praying out loud, something that I could never have done. And ever since the night I saw big, tough Bill Hull pray at the Christmas service, I have wondered how it was that Bill—and now Larry—could do that and I couldn't. It's a question that I'm still trying to answer.

Ultimately, Larry's prayers were not enough to save his marriage. But before he and Jonelle went their separate ways, they produced a wonderful child by the name of Geoff, who transformed their brief relationship into a sterling example of how God works in mysterious ways.

The Franks' Valentine's Day Party

Larry married a second time, this time happily, and he and his new wife, Ulrike, asked us to play for a Valentine's Day party at their home. But the Franks' party has a couple of wonderful backstories that need to be told first. The first of these has to do with their courtship—if you could call it that—and the second has to do with the reason for the party.

Although Larry and I never talked about it, the failure of his first marriage had shaken him. Larry was not used to failing. His life had been about succeeding, most often in grand style, so how could he have made such an obvious mistake when it came to selecting a mate?

And to add insult to injury, after their separation Jonelle had moved back to Eugene, and every other weekend Larry was forced to travel between Portland and Eugene a total of four times—436 miles—to be with his son, an ordeal that Larry found both irksome and demeaning.

In 1982, Ulrike Meyer was a twenty-two-year-old German-born nursing student at the Walla Walla College School of Nursing, which was located on the campus of the Portland Adventist Medical Center. She was tall, blonde, and attractive, as well as bright, industrious, and devout.

Ulrike was the only child of a single mother, and when she was five, she and her mother immigrated to the United States. Although they settled in New York City, they moved to Eugene when Ulrike was thirteen.

Once she was in nursing school, when Ulrike wasn't working or otherwise occupied, she tried to visit her mother on weekends. But money was tight and her car was undependable, so getting to Eugene wasn't always possible.

When Ulrike first saw the thirty-nine-year-old neurosurgeon she would later marry, he was featured in an educational film that the nursing school had made to teach neurosurgical nursing. In the film, Dr. Franks was standing in his scrubs and lecturing to the camera. Although the class had been told that Dr. Franks was also a member of the Adventist Medical Center staff, the man that Ulrike saw on the screen didn't fit her image of a neurosurgeon. In her mind, a neurosurgeon should be older and smaller than this Dr. Franks, who looked both too young and too big to be operating on people's brains.

The first time Ulrike saw Dr. Franks in person, she and her friend Gabrielle were in a shopping center. The Dr. Franks she knew from the nursing film was now dressed in a sport coat and tie and was standing outside an automatic photo booth with a boy of three or four who Ulrike guessed must be his son. As soon as she recognized Dr. Franks, both girls stepped behind a sign so they could watch undetected.

Dr. Franks was trying to coax the boy into the photo booth, but the boy was protesting, and there were tears. But despite the boy's distress, Ulrike couldn't take her eyes off of Dr. Franks, who in person seemed even bigger than he had in the teaching film.

"Look at that neck!" she whispered to Gabrielle. "Have you ever seen a neck like that before?"

THE LOVEHANDLES

The reason for her amazement was that athletes, both former—like Dr. Franks—and current, were unknown to Ulrike, who had never played sports or attended an athletic event. Fascinated by the size and shape of Dr. Franks, she continued watching until he and his son had left the mall.

Then in February of 1983, Ulrike was doing a rotation through the intensive care unit and the recovery room and had been instructed to deliver a message to one of the recovery room nurses. While Ulrike was standing at the nursing station delivering the message, Dr. Franks entered the room. When their eyes met, Ulrike felt electricity pass between them. It was a powerful and unforgettable sensation, and the startled look on Dr. Franks' face told Ulrike that he had felt it too.

A few days later Ulrike had entered the ICU at 6:45 a.m. for morning report, and in Bed 2 she saw an Asian man lying on a cooling blanket, shivering violently but without a stitch of clothing on. Even his genitalia were uncovered. A sign above his bed identified him as a patient of Dr. Franks.

As a foreign-born person, Ulrike was incensed that the nurses could treat another foreigner with such indifference. But when the patient in Bed 2 came up for discussion in morning report, it was clear that much of their apparent neglect was because the nurses didn't know much about him, and without knowing his history, his ability to communicate, or his prognosis, they had been unable to formulate a proper treatment plan.

Following morning report, Ulrike and the staff nurses attended to the patients: bathing them, dressing them in fresh gowns, and changing their bedding. Then Dr. Franks entered the ICU, took a seat, and began looking through his patients' charts. After a moment of indecision, Ulrike decided to speak to him about the patient in Bed 2.

Gathering her courage, she said, "Dr. Franks, I think that the man in Bed 2 might get better care if the nurses knew more about him."

Although it had seemed like a reasonable request to Ulrike, to her surprise, Dr. Franks stood and in a loud, stern voice said, "Nurses are professionals, and I do not give pep talks to nurses!"

Not only had Ulrike been chastised, but she was certain that the other nurses had heard his outburst and would be upset with her for making him angry. She apologized quickly and waited for the nurses to descend on her, but thankfully no one came.

Finally Dr. Franks began making rounds with both the nurses and Ulrike in attendance. At Bed 2, Dr. Franks stopped and explained that this gentleman, who was Vietnamese, had been in a motorcycle accident six months before, and after an extended hospitalization had been discharged to a rehabilitation center.

Then Dr. Franks put his fingers inside the man's hand and asked him to squeeze as hard as he could, and the man responded by doing exactly that. Then he told the man to squeeze once if he meant "yes" and twice if he meant "no," and followed that with a series of questions that required a "yes" or "no" answer. To Ulrike's surprise, the man answered all of the questions correctly.

Then Dr. Franks leaned over the bed and explained to the man that he had an infection, but that the infection could be treated with antibiotics, and when he was better he would return to the rehabilitation center to continue working toward his recovery.

Ulrike was elated. Now there could be no doubt that this man, who was both expressionless and unable to speak, had understood everything that Dr. Franks had said, and armed with the information that Dr. Franks had just given them, the nurses would be able to take better care of him. And she was perhaps most impressed with Dr. Franks, who had not only done everything that she had asked, but he had done it with such kindness.

Dr. Franks then completed his rounds and wrote progress notes in all his patients' charts. As he was preparing to leave the unit, Ulrike heard him tell one of the nurses, "I'm so excited because this weekend I'll be with my son, Geoffrey. He lives in Eugene and I go there to see him every other weekend."

And suddenly Ulrike heard herself saying, "You know, my mother lives in Eugene, and my VW doesn't do very well on the freeway. I've been taking the bus, but do you think that I could ride with you sometime?"

Her request had been so shockingly inappropriate that Ulrike couldn't believe that she had said it. And Dr. Franks, who looked every bit as startled as she felt, had said, "Call my office," and rushed out of the ICU.

Two months later Ulrike called his office, and after convincing his secretary that Dr. Franks had really told her to call when she needed a ride to Eugene, was eventually instructed to meet him at his office at 2:00 p.m. on Friday afternoon.

What followed their trip to Eugene was an off-and-on relationship that lasted for two and a half years, and most of the time felt to Ulrike like it was going nowhere. But in September of 1985, Larry was scheduled to go on a fishing trip to the Queen Charlotte Islands with George Sample, George's two sons, and some other men. A few days before they were to leave, Larry was telling Ulrike how beautiful it was in British Columbia this time of year and how much fun the trip would be.

"Gosh, Uli," he said, "I wish you could go fishing with us."

And Ulrike had replied, "Well, if I came with you, we'd have to be married."

"Well, then let's get married," Larry had said, but stated it so offhandedly that she wasn't sure if he meant it or not. But he had said it nonetheless, and Ulrike decided that she would test his intentions.

The next day Ulrike called the county office of records and inquired about the procedure for getting married by a judge. She was told that after submitting their application for a marriage license, a couple had to wait at least three days before a judge could marry them. By Ulrike's calculations, if she submitted the papers tomorrow, they could be married on the same day that they were to leave for the fishing trip. So she went to the courthouse and got the application form, and the following day, with no advance warning, she waited in the hallway outside of the operating room where Larry was finishing a case.

When Larry left the operating room, he was surprised to see Ulrike standing in the hall. "Hey, Uli, what's up?" he asked.

Ulrike replied, "Well, if you're still serious about getting married so that I can go fishing with you, here's the application for the marriage license," and handed him the papers.

Larry looked like he had just been kicked in the stomach, and blurted out, "Are you really serious about this, Ulrike? You're not going to change your mind, are you? I mean, you're really young. Do you think you can always love me?"

To which Ulrike had answered, "Yes, I'm serious. No, I'm not going to change my mind. And yes, I will always love you."

Then Larry, still looking confused, said, "I'm sorry, Uli, just give me a minute to think about this." But in less than a minute, an enormous smile spread across his face, and he said, "Okay, Uli, let's get married," and using the top of a gurney as a desk, he signed the marriage papers.

The following Monday, Larry and Ulrike met Ulrike's maid of honor—my partner's wife, Letha Figg-Hoblyn—as well as George Sample and his two boys in Judge Mercedes Diaz's office. The entire wedding party wore jeans, and in addition, the bride wore the groom's father's red plaid wool shirt. Immediately after the ceremony, the group caravanned to Vancouver, BC, and took a small plane to the Queen Charlotte Islands.

Once they returned from Canada, their lives became a whirlwind of activity. Within two weeks Ulrike was pregnant, and in early October, Larry and Ulrike flew to Chicago so Larry could attend a meeting of the Neurosurgical Congress, and the twenty-five-year-old Ulrike, now suffering from morning sickness, did her best to fit in with the other, older wives.

Then later that same October, Larry went on a hunting trip during which he became separated from his party and spent a snowy, subzero night alone in the Montana wilderness. And after leaving Larry at the airport for the hunting trip, Ulrike had narrowly escaped a head-on collision with a truck on an icy Oregon highway as she was driving to Spokane to get their new German wire-haired pointer puppy.

But in between their near-death experiences and the holidays, they had been thinking about how they might celebrate their marriage, and decided to host a Valentine's Day party for their friends with music provided by the Lovehandles.

Ulrike, who readily admits that she knew nothing about popular music, remembers that she asked me if the band could play something from *The Sound of Music* and *Fiddler on the Roof*. Apparently I had responded with a look that said, "Really, Ulrike? Seriously?" But then we had played one or two selections from *The Sound of Music*, as well as "Sunrise, Sunset" from *Fiddler on the Roof*. The party was the perfect way for Larry and Ulrike to celebrate their new life together.

The Gigs Keep Coming

Following the Valentine's Day party, we played a wedding and a graduation party, and after a six-month hiatus we played another dance at the Oregon Yacht Club, this time for an organization called the Brim Association.

The Brim Association managed a number of small hospitals throughout the western half of the United States. Although large hospitals in large cities always hired their own management teams, small hospitals were often in locations where the personnel needed to run a hospital—the CEOs, CFOs, human resource managers, medical and nursing supervisors, and support service (x-ray, laboratory, physical therapy, and occupational therapy) managers—were simply not available. And in those instances, companies like the Brim Association were hired to supply those services long distance.

It was an interesting concept, and not one that I had been familiar with before we played the gig. But like most company parties we had played, the Brim party felt self-conscious and restrained, and it was not nearly as much fun as the first party we played at the Oregon Yacht Club.

The Irvington Club

On September 20, 1986, we played a dance for the Irvington Community Association in the ballroom of the Irvington Club.

The Irvington neighborhood was one of the oldest, most beautiful, and most interesting in Portland. It was located in the northeast part of the city within a rectangle formed by Fremont and Broadway streets on the north and south, and Northeast 26th and 7th Streets on the east and west. Construction of the district began in 1891 and continued through the first half of the twentieth century. The homes there were a mix of Victorian, Queen Anne, Arts and Crafts, Craftsman, Colonial Revival, Prairie, and Bungalow styles, and many of them were magnificent.

Although Irvington began as one of Portland's wealthier neighborhoods, over time it became a working-class neighborhood. In 1966 the Irvington Community Association was formed to promote and preserve this historic old district.

In keeping with the neighborhood's affluent beginnings, the Irvington Club was founded in 1898 as a tennis club whose purpose was "to share among our members a love of tennis that is distinguished by friendliness, inclusiveness, and tradition." Over one hundred years later, it was still one of Portland's most prestigious athletic clubs.

The Irvington Club's stately Craftsman clubhouse was built in 1912, and although it was an honor to play in such a historic building in such a historic neighborhood, setting up for the event became a headache of historic dimensions. As wonderful as the old clubhouse was, it was not designed with rock-and-roll bands in mind, and we spent several frantic hours before the party trying to find a combination of electrical outlets that would power our equipment without blowing fuses. Eventually we did, and to our amazement, the party went off without a hitch.

THE LOVEHANDLES

Rose City Sound and Lighting

After the Irvington Club, most of our jobs required a sound technician. By then we were playing larger venues where the sound had to be mixed to fit the acoustics of the room and then adjusted for the number of people on the dance floor. In addition to larger rooms, the venues had gotten nicer, and we were being paid proportionally more for playing them. The Franks' party would be the last house party we would ever play.

For big jobs, the mixing board was positioned at the back of the hall, which meant that someone separate from the band had to operate it. Although Warner Swarner had done this for us in Portland, on the road we needed someone besides Warner.

Our first gig after the Irvington Club was another OMGMA party, this time at the Salishan Resort, which was 110 miles from Portland on the Oregon coast. The lodge was as beautiful as any place we would ever play, and the room where we would be playing was large enough to require a soundman.

We began our search by calling some of the local sound companies, and hit pay dirt almost immediately. Rose City Sound and Lighting said that they could supply us with an experienced sound technician at a very reasonable price, and for a few dollars more we could get lights and a second technician to run them. We couldn't say yes fast enough.

Several times in the past we had rented small arrays of stage lights that ran on automatic timers and changed colors every few seconds, and we had always felt that they were a nice addition to our parties. Although by now we had enough sound equipment to play almost anywhere, we were reluctant to buy our own lighting. Lights were big and bulky, and just one more pain in the ass to deal with.

The Salishan party turned out to be a wonderful experience. The OMGMA partygoers were once again enthusiastic and fun, the two technicians were personable and professional, the sound and lighting perfect. In addition, they had transported all the equipment (both ours and theirs), set it up, and then taken care of all of the niggling little problems that invariably crop up during a performance and require immediate attention. But best of all, they seemed to enjoy working with us. We came away from the party very impressed with Rose City Sound and Lighting and were looking forward to using them again.

CHAPTER 16: THE BIG PROBLEM

31. April 23, 1987—OMGMA Party at Rippling River Resort
32. August 25, 1987—Oregon Academy of Family Practice Party
33. October 24, 1987—Mount Hood Medical Center
    Benefit at the Columbia Gorge Hotel
34. December 15, 1987—Precision Castparts Corporation
    Christmas Party at the Waverly Country Club
35. February 27, 1988—Suburban Medical Clinic Party
36. April 30, 1988—Our third Oregon Academy of Family
    Practice Meeting, this time at the Valley River Inn in Eugene
37. August 6, 1988—McMahon Wedding
38. December 10, 1988—Pacificare of Oregon Christmas Party
    at the Oregon Home Builders Association Center
39. January 21, 1989—Mount Hood Medical Society Banquet
    at the Columbia Red Lion's Riverview Ballroom
40. April 1, 1989—April Fool's Day Party at the
    Oregon Home Builders Association Center

The first party of 1987 was our third OMGMA dance, which like the two previous parties was a night of wild, dance-filled fun, proving once again that they were far and away the best group we ever played for.

Then in August we played a second dance for the Oregon Academy of Family Practice, and although it was obviously an important gig, I have no memory of it. But perhaps the memory was simply swept away by the storm that was about to break.

The Lovehandles

Mike's Dilemma

Overall, Mike was very pleased with the band. He had taken a new job in a new city, and the Lovehandles had welcomed him into their lives and become his friends. And though it was nothing that he felt needed saying, many times his bandmates had, in fact, told him how happy they were to have him in the band.

And the band was doing well. We had found a niche playing private parties, most often for people and organizations within the medical community, and our popularity was growing. And though the band was far from perfect, everyone worked hard, and the results were enjoyed and appreciated by our audiences. It was hard to argue with success.

Though Mike was as important to the band's success as anyone in the band, there was no doubt that Patti was its leader. For in addition to asking for everyone's input and being absolutely fair in her decisions, Patti was the ultimate decision-maker, and that, as far as Mike could tell, was just fine with everyone, himself included.

And in addition to her managerial skills, there was also no doubt that Patti was the one who made the band go. She was a master at motivating a crowd, at getting people out onto the dance floor and enjoying themselves. And though audiences could sometimes be difficult, Patti seemed to enjoy the challenge. Mike may have been the better musician, but he was simply too reserved to energize a party like Patti.

But as important as she was to the band's success, Patti's singing could be flat—not always, but much of the time—and that bothered Mike. In fact, it bothered him a lot, and under their current system of sharing vocals, it was inescapable. There were no songs in the band's play list that he or Patti sang alone. When Mike sang lead, Patti harmonized, or tried to, and when Patti sang lead, Mike harmonized. But when they were singing together, there was often a degree of dissonance. Although this was less obvious when the backup vocals were sung softly, Mike still noticed it. And despite doing his absolute best to ignore the dissonance

180

and appreciate the overall effect that their music was having on the audience, he could not shut it out of his mind.

Mike was a perfectionist, and although he could deal with most varieties of imperfection, vocal dissonance wasn't one of them. Ever since the fourth grade when he was tapped on the shoulder and asked to join the school choir, Mike had loved harmony. In high school he sang in the school choir, two folk ensembles, and a barbershop quartet: all groups depending on harmony. At Riverside Mike had joined the elite university choir, where harmony was no longer a goal but a requirement, and before joining the Lovehandles, he had sung with a barbershop quartet. His entire musical history was, in fact, more about vocal harmony than it was any other aspect of music.

Mike didn't need a band to be happy—he was just fine singing by himself or with his guitar—but if he were singing with others, their voices had to blend. It was an absolute necessity. It was his line in the sand.

Mike knew that he was alone in this. As far as he knew, no one had ever complained about Patti's vocals. People came to their parties to have fun; musical perfection was not a requirement. Nor had his bandmates expressed any dissatisfaction with Patti's vocals. No, this was Mike's problem, and he would have to deal with it on his own. But his choices for doing so were limited: either he had to live with the fact that she would intermittently be flat, Patti would have to learn to sing on key, or they would have to stop singing together.

Two of these three options could be eliminated immediately. First, his ability to tolerate her vocals was not going to improve with time. He knew himself too well to consider that a real possibility. And telling Patti that they could no longer sing together was too dangerous. If she saw this as an insult, it could destroy the band. No, his only real choice—at least for now—was to make Patti aware of the problem and hope that she could fix it.

Giving people bad news was probably Mike's least favorite thing to do, but Patti had been surprisingly receptive to being told that she was sometimes flat. Although she had not noticed it herself, she accepted the news with surprising grace and had even asked how she might correct it.

THE LOVEHANDLES

Mike told her what he knew. Singing flat, he said, often occurred because the singer's voice resonated in the chest instead of in the head where it could best be heard, and if a singer were to relax the muscles of their mouth, throat, and face so that the facial cavities rather than the chest became the voice's sounding board, the singer's pitch would often rise. What he didn't say was that Patti's success would depend on whether or not she could hear the difference. Because if she couldn't, the problem could not be corrected.

Patti tried. He had to give her that. Over the next several practices she remained conscious of where her voice was resonating, and would periodically ask Mike if her pitch were better. Although he always said that it was, her improvement was minimal at best.

With our gig at the Columbia Gorge Hotel approaching, we again called Rose City Sound and Lighting to request the lights and the two technicians that we had used in the past. At prior jobs, Mark, the Rose City sound technician, had mentioned that our sound might be improved by using one of their new mixing boards instead of our own. But because renting another piece of equipment cost more money, we had always said no. But this time when we called and Mark made his pitch for trying one of their new boards, for no good reason we said sure, bring one of your boards.

The reason behind Mark's interest in using one of their new boards was that he, too, was aware of Patti's problem, and the new mixing boards had the capacity to correct pitch. Each of the board's channels had a knob that could be turned up or down to adjust the pitch of its input, and he was anxious to try this on Patti's vocals.

After the party, Mark handed Mike a tape that he had recorded during our performance and confessed that he had recommended the new board because he wanted to see if it could correct Patti's pitch. But, he said, Patti's problem was intermittent, and though raising her pitch helped when she was flat, it made her sharp when she was singing on key. And to illustrate the difference between the corrected and the uncorrected versions of her singing, Mark had adjusted her pitch on the first half of the tape, but left it uncorrected on the second

182

half. He suggested that Mike listen to the tape and draw his own conclusions. If Mike thought that the adjustment had been helpful, we could continue using their boards, but if not, then our board was adequate.

Mike took the tape home and listened to it several times. Because of the variability of her pitch, neither version of Patti's voice sounded much better than the other. But more disturbing than her pitch was Mike's discovery that when they sang together, it was often difficult to tell whose voice was off, and the thought that he might be blamed for Patti's problem was very bothersome to him. But the larger issue was that despite her own efforts and the aid of current technology, Patti's pitch could not be corrected. Now Mike needed a good plan B, and he didn't have one.

One evening Mike called me to discuss his dilemma. The anguish in his voice told me that the current situation was unacceptable and that something had to be done. But what? After explaining what they had already tried, it seemed like his options were down to one: Mike and Patti could no longer sing together. I tried to think of something else he could do, but I couldn't, and ended the conversation by saying that I would support him whatever he decided to do.

The Columbia Gorge Hotel and Spa

Completed in 1922, the Historic Columbia River Highway was America's first planned scenic highway. It was a beautiful seventy-five-mile stretch of road running along the Columbia River between Portland and a town to the east of Portland called The Dalles.

Also completed in 1922 was the highway's destination spot, the magnificent Columbia Gorge Hotel. Standing amid seven acres of gardens and waterfalls, the hotel had originally been designed as a retreat for the rich and famous.

But financial problems had ensued, and between 1925 and 1952 the hotel changed ownership several times and wound up as a retirement home. Then in 1978 the property was sold once again, and following a million-dollar renovation, it opened a year later as a 42-room luxury hotel and spa.

The dance that we would be playing there was a fundraiser for the Mount Hood Medical Center, a medical complex in Gresham, Oregon, a city on the eastern outskirts of Portland. The dance would be our first benefit concert, which seemed like an important step for us. But while Mike was fretting about Patti's pitch, another problem developed in the lead-up to the dance. This time, it involved Les.

Following their divorce, Cheryl sold their Portland home, and she and the kids had moved back to Pittsburgh, where she bought the old Andrew Mellon residence. In the midst of the band's preparation for the Columbia Gorge Hotel gig, Les had decided to visit his children in Pittsburgh.

The Andrew Mellon house was a huge Victorian mansion with a maze of floors, rooms, and hallways that were completely unfamiliar to Les. One evening as he was searching the main floor for a bathroom, he opened what he thought was the bathroom door. The room was completely dark. Thinking that there must be a light switch on the right-hand wall, Les took one step into the darkness and found himself falling down a steep flight of stairs into the basement. Lying stunned on the basement floor, he took inventory and discovered that his left wrist was broken. He called for help, but Cheryl and the kids had heard him fall, and had already called for an ambulance. At the hospital his wrist was x-rayed, set, and put into a cast that covered his left forearm and hand down to the base of his fingers.

At his first band practice after returning home from Pittsburgh, Les arrived late, holding his left arm in the air for all of us to see. We immediately stopped what we were doing and stared at him.

"Hi, guys," he said sheepishly. "When I was in Pittsburgh, I, uh . . . fell down some stairs . . . and broke my wrist."

We knew what was coming, and we were furious. How could Les have been so careless as to break his goddamned wrist right before such an important gig? He was a critical part of the band, and many of the songs that we had been practicing featured piano solos that only he could play. Now here he was about to tell us that he couldn't play them.

"I'm sorry," he continued, "but I'm afraid I won't be able to play at the Columbia Gorge Hotel. I'm really sorry. I—"

Then something inside me snapped and I shot back, "That's bullshit, Les. We can't play this gig without you, and it's too late to cancel."

Les smiled weakly and waved his arm around some more, as though I might have missed his injury the first time.

"See the cast?" he said. "I can't move my wrist, and if I can't move my wrist, I can't play the piano. If I tried, the cast would just bang on the keys. I'm sorry, but I can't play. You'll have to make other arrangements."

Other arrangements? What other arrangements were we going to make? Now we were really pissed.

Then Patti answered, "So what should we do, Les? Call Van Cliburn and ask him to sit in for you? You have two hands, don't you? So use the other hand."

And Bart added, "Les, I can see your fingers poking out of the cast, and unless I'm mistaken, piano players play with their fingers, not their wrists!"

Les tried once more to convince us that he couldn't play, but we wouldn't listen and kept piling on the crap until he sat down behind the keyboard and said that he'd give it a try.

Although his playing wasn't perfect, it was good enough. We were, after all, the Lovehandles; mistakes were just part of the experience.

Our performance at the Columbia Gorge Hotel dance, was, with one small exception, no better or worse than usual. That exception occurred during one of Les's piano solos when he reached for a note with his left hand and fell off the piano stool. But the band picked up the melody and someone picked up Les, and we finished the song—and I don't think that anyone noticed.

We quit around midnight, and by 1:00 a.m. we had packed all our stuff into the technicians' van, walked to our cars, and driven off.

185

But the drive from the Columbia Gorge Hotel back to Portland was more than sixty miles, and after a while Les began to feel sleepy. Thinking that he should stop and have a cup of coffee, he turned off the highway at a truck stop, locked his car, and went inside. When he returned to his car, he couldn't find his keys—but looking through the car window, he saw them still in the ignition. He thought of calling the AAA emergency number but wondered how long it would take them to get there. It could be quite a while.

No; it was late, Les was tired, and he wasn't going to spend another hour waiting for AAA. Instead, he walked to the service station and asked to borrow a tire iron. Then he went to his car, shattered a side window, opened the door, brushed the glass off the seat, and drove home.

It was just another day in the life of Les Naman.

The Announcement

We followed the Columbia Gorge Hotel party with a Christmas dance for the Precision Castparts Corporation at the Waverly Country Club and a dance for Bart McMullan's office, the Suburban Medical Clinic.

Our next job was a dance for the Oregon Academy of Family Practice at the Valley River Inn in Eugene. A few weeks before the dance, we were in Les's basement preparing for the gig. We had just finished playing the first set and were taking a short break before tackling the second when suddenly, in a faint, uncertain voice, Mike said that he had something to tell us.

He began by saying that he had made a decision, and that it hadn't been an easy one. There was a problem, he said, with the band's vocals, and though some of us might not see it as much of a problem, it was upsetting to him. The problem, he said, was that at times Patti's voice was flat so that when they harmonized, it made both their voices sound off key. He said that he had been aware of this for some time, and though he had tried to ignore it, he couldn't. A few weeks ago he had told Patti about the problem, and she had tried to correct it, but she hadn't been successful. As a result, the only way that he knew of dealing with it was for Patti not to sing when he sang lead. If she wanted him to continue singing backup when she sang lead, that would be fine, but from now on she had to stop singing when he sang lead. And if the rest of the band thought that this was unacceptable, he would be willing to leave the band.

A shocked silence had followed. It was Mike saying the words, "I would be willing to leave the band" that hit us the hardest. Although the Lovehandles were a band before Mike's arrival, there was no doubt that he had made us better, and the thought of not having him in the band was unsettling to say the least. Although each of us had some trouble understanding how Patti's vocals could be so unacceptable as to warrant his declaration, we knew that Mike would not have said it if it wasn't true. As our only "real musician," his musical standards were undoubtedly higher than ours.

But left hanging was the question of how Patti felt about this. She had just been told that she had to stop singing when Mike sang lead, and as the de facto leader of the band, could she accept this? In the confusion that followed Mike's announcement, I had either missed her response, or she hadn't said anything—which for Patti would have been unusual. Patti was not one to remain silent on matters involving the band, and if Mike had said something that she thought was unacceptable, we would have heard about it. But we hadn't. And when I looked at Patti, she didn't look angry; she just looked embarrassed, which I took to mean that she had accepted it.

My own reaction to Mike's statement was equally unexpected: his criticism of Patti made me acutely aware of my own musical shortcomings. Mike had just criticized Patti, who along with Mike was one of our stars. If Mike could find fault with Patti, couldn't he just as easily have found fault with the rest of us? Well, maybe not Tom. Although Tom was no Eric Clapton, he was a competent musician. But besides Tom, couldn't Mike have criticized Bart, or Les, or me? I had no doubt that the answer to that was yes.

But in the context of our band, Mike's words felt oddly out of place, and at first I wondered why. But then it occurred to me that in the eight years of our existence—and the thousands of musical blunders that we had made in front of each other—the one thing we had never done was criticize one another, which in our situation seemed like an absolute necessity. To play publicly was to open yourself up to criticism, and as precarious as our musical abilities were, we needed all the support we could get.

Many times when the Lovehandles had walked out onstage to begin a performance, the feeling that I had reminded me of those times in grade school when you were given the task of standing up in front of your classmates, teachers, and parents and singing a song or reciting a poem. A day or two before your big performance, you were at home practicing with your mother, and you were terrified. Terrified! Then you got the words mixed up, and you fell apart. You began crying and you told your mom that you didn't want to do it, that you *couldn't* do it, that you would rather die first. But then your mom had put her arms around you, and said that you were going to be just fine, that she had never heard anyone sing that song or recite that poem any better than you, and that you were going to do a wonderful job.

And it had helped. You stopped crying and you tried again, and this time you did okay. And when you finally got up on the stage and did your bit, you might not have put yourself in contention for a Grammy or a Tony, but you did well enough. You survived.

It was that kind of support that we had given each other. Collectively we had created an atmosphere of acceptance that helped us perform. And now that feeling was gone, and though Mike's words had been directed at Patti, they made the rest of us feel vulnerable and replaceable too. And it wasn't a good feeling.

My memory of what happened next is hazy. Tom, who was always our greatest advocate, may have said that Patti and Mike were both good vocalists, and he was not aware of any problem with the way they sounded. Les might have said that he missed some of what Mike just told us and would he please go through it again. And Bart probably reassured Patti and the rest of us that although Mike's request had come as a shock, the Lovehandles would recover and life would go on.

But the one thing that no one had said was that Mike was wrong. Although many of us, like Tom, had not been aware of the problem before, at some level we knew that Mike was probably right. But knowing that didn't help, and no matter who had said what, everything was different now. The band had been mortally wounded, and its future was uncertain.

Patti Struggles

Patti felt blindsided. Weeks before, when she and Mike talked about her pitch, Mike had presented it as a minor issue. And though Patti silently questioned his assertion that she was sometimes flat, she had gone along with it and even asked what she could do to make it better. Then she had done everything that Mike suggested, and whenever she asked him if her pitch were better, he had always said that it was. But if that were true, whatever pitch problems she may or may not have had should have been resolved—and now Mike was saying that they weren't. In fact, he was saying that her pitch was so bad that they couldn't sing together. Obviously he hadn't been telling her the truth.

But did she really have a pitch problem? Patti found that hard to believe. Not only could she not hear the problem herself, but in all the years that she had been singing—with her sister, with the Sweet Adelines, in her church choir, and with the Lovehandles—no one except Mike had ever accused her of being flat. In fact, people had always praised her singing. So could all those people have been wrong and Mike be right? It didn't make any sense. And if she really didn't have a pitch problem, why would Mike say that she did? Jealousy? Spite? No, Mike wouldn't do that. Would he?

But right or wrong, Mike's announcement made her mad. Even if she was a little flat from time to time, was that reason enough to relegate her to a secondary position within the band? Although Mike may have been the better singer, wasn't she the one who made the band go? The one who made their parties fun? And hadn't she welcomed Mike into the band and insisted that he be an equal partner in selecting their songs and singing lead? And now he was saying that she couldn't sing with him? It wasn't fair, and it pissed her off.

But God, did it hurt. The Lovehandles were her band, so much so that people had often called them "Patti and the Lovehandles"—and with good reason. She had worked her butt off for the band, and now everyone was siding with Mike. Well, maybe not siding, but certainly no one had jumped up to say that Mike was wrong.

And now when Mike was singing, what was she supposed to do? Keep her mouth shut and do what? Tap her tambourine? Part of the band's success had been due to her spontaneity and her enthusiasm, and now she was to sing at certain specified times only. So what was she going to do when Mike was singing? Stand in the background, smile, and at the end of the song tell the audience, "Thanks Mike, that was really great!" And what if she forgot and sang along with him when she wasn't supposed to? Would he chastise her in front of the band or in front of the audience? No, he'd probably just shoot her a look that said, "Please, don't do that again"—but that would be bad enough.

What Bart saw happening to Patti worried him. Following Mike's announcement, there had been a dramatic change in her disposition. The band, which had formerly given Patti such joy, was now causing her pain. It was as though the band was her baby and Mike had been granted custody, or that she had just been diagnosed with an incurable illness and was now working through the stages of grief. Although other things in her life—their home; her work; and her daughter, Amy—might distract her for a while, her thoughts always returned to the band.

Bart had tried to help her. They had discussed the situation over and over until there was nothing new to say, and then they had discussed it some more. Many times he had told her that he would do whatever she wanted. The band had had a good run, and maybe it was time to quit.

But as much as the situation rankled, Patti wasn't ready to quit. She would wait to see what happened. She'd keep working on her pitch and maybe it would improve, or maybe Mike would have a change of heart. Stranger things have happened. In the meantime, she would abide by the rules and be silent when Mike sang lead. It sounded so simple, but it was so damned hard.

And the Band Played On

On April 3, 1988, we played a third dance for the Oregon Academy of Family Practice, this time at the Valley River Inn in Eugene. Although a feeling of uneasiness hung in the air, we did our best to ignore it. On August 6 we played a wedding, and on December 10 we played a party for Pacificare of Oregon.

Founded in 1975, Pacificare was one of the first health plans on the West Coast to qualify as a managed care organization. The cost of healthcare had risen dramatically, and Bart McMullan was one of the first physicians in Oregon to recognize that this had to be curbed. As a result, he had toyed with the idea of switching from being a full-time physician—a job that he both loved and was very good at—to working within the medical insurance industry, where he might have a greater impact on the future of medicine. Bart thought that managed care offered promise, and in 1985 his and three other Portland medical offices opened Pacificare's first subsidiary outside of California. He was now working there one afternoon a week as its medical director, and as a result of his new job, he'd gotten us the gig.

One of the nicest features of the Pacificare party was where it was held, which was at the Oregon Home Builders Association center. Located just off I-5, the main north-south freeway running through the city, the building was one of those attractive but unlabeled structures that caught your eye as you drove past and left you wondering what it was for. Relatively new and conveniently located, it had a nice stage and a large dance floor, and though it was neither as grand nor as beautiful as some of the other places we'd played, all things considered it was a great place for a party. Although no one in the band had ever mentioned that we might be on the verge of breaking up, I think that we all filed the Oregon Home Builders Association away as a good place to play a final gig, if it ever came to that.

Although there had been no further discussion of the new singing arrangements, the atmosphere at both band practices and gigs felt tense and uncertain. Even our relationships with one another felt different, as though the rules governing our friendships had changed and we no longer knew how to act around each other.

And instead of riding the wave of joy that I usually felt playing the drums, I was constantly aware of my deficiencies. Although I still loved the drums, my inability to keep a solid beat, play interesting and professional-sounding drum fills, and construct a decent drum solo were always on my mind. As a musical entity, the band felt stagnant, and that wasn't what I wanted. More than anything, I wanted us to get better. I wanted to be a good drummer in a good band, and that, I feared, would never happen with the Lovehandles.

My picture of the band's future was unclear. There seemed to be two possible paths we could take, but whether Mike's announcement would lead to positive change within the band or its dissolution, I didn't know. It was just too early to tell.

The April Fool's Day Dance

In January of 1989 we played a dance for the Mount Hood Medical Society in the Riverview Ballroom of the Columbia Red Lion, and though the party had been a success, it had been a struggle. The joy of playing was simply gone.

Then someone in the band suggested that we rent the Oregon Home Builders Association center and throw a party for our families, friends, and office staffs, many of whom had never seen us play. We called the center and found that it was available on April 1, 1989, so we booked the date. We would host an April Fool's Day Party.

Although we never talked about this show as our swan song, on some level I'm sure that's how we saw it. It would not *necessarily* be our last performance, but just in case it was, we wanted to thank all the people who had so unselfishly supported us for the last ten years.

Then while we were busy planning and practicing for the April Fool's Day party, something unexpected happened: we were asked to play a dinner dance in November for the city's largest medical group, Kaiser Permanente, and because we had never discussed breaking up, we accepted the job. So now we would need to continue practicing even after the April Fool's Day Party.

But we ignored the Kaiser gig and threw ourselves into preparations for the April party. We used all the knowledge that we had gleaned from ten years of playing other people's parties into planning our own. Mike added several new songs to the set list, and we practiced harder than we had in a long time. And when April 1 finally rolled around, we put on a great party—one of our best. Our guests had a wonderful time, and everyone danced. But though it had been a huge success, there was an undeniable sadness to it, as well.

April Fool's Day Dance Set List

Set One
1. "Soolaiman," by Neil Diamond (Mike)
2. Neil Diamond Medley: "Thank the Lord for the Night Time" and "Cherry, Cherry" (Mike)
3. "Dream Weaver," by Gary Wright (Patti)
4. "Wake Up Little Susie," by the Everly Brothers (Mike)
5. Fifties Medley (unfortunately no one can remember the songs)
6. "Keep Your Hands to Yourself," by The Georgia Satellites (Mike)
7. "Baby Don't Go," Sonny and Cher (it's unclear who sang this)
8. "Old Time Rock and Roll," by Bob Seger (Mike)
9. "Can't Help Falling in Love," as sung by Elvis Presley (Mike)
10. "Cry Myself to Sleep," by the Judds (Patti)

11. "Kansas City," as sung by Wilbert Harrison (Mike)
12. "I Want to Know What Love Is," by Foreigner (Patti)
13. "Let It Roll," by the band Little Feat (Mike)

Set Two

14. Medley: "Devil with the Blue Dress," by Mitch Ryder and the Detroit Wheels; "Good Golly, Miss Molly," by Little Richard; "See See Rider," traditional song first recorded by Gertrude "Ma" Rainey; and "Jenny, Jenny," by Little Richard (Mike)
15. "Walk of Life," by Dire Straits (Mike)
16. "Jailhouse Rock," as sung by Elvis Presley (Mike)
17. Buddy Holly Medley: "Everyday" and "Oh Boy!" (Mike)
18. "Bop," —as sung by Dan Seals (Mike).
19. "Nobody Does It Better," written by Marvin Hamlisch and Carole Bayer Sager, and sung by Carly Simon (Patti)
20. Dance Contest: "(Do) The Twist," "Limbo Rock," and "Rock Around the Clock." ("The Twist" was written by Hank Ballard (of Hank Ballard and the Midnighters— remember Camp Lincoln?), "Limbo Rock" was written by Kal Mann and Billy Strange, and both songs were made popular by Chubby Checker. Rock Around the Clock was the number one hit in the nation in 1955 for Bill Haley and the Comets. Patti sang Limbo Rock and Mike sang the other two songs,
21. "Peggy Sue," by Buddy Holly (Mike)
22. "Please Be the One," by Karla Bonoff (Patti)
23. "La Bamba," by Ritchie Valens (Mike)
24. "Wipe Out," by The Surfaris (drum solo by Bob)
25. "It's Too Late," by Carole King (Patti)
26. *Proud Mary,"* by John Fogerty, as sung by Tina Turner (Patti)

Set Three

27. "Gimme Some Lovin'," by the Spencer Davis Group (Mike)
28. "Louie, Louie," by Richard Berry as sung by The Kingsmen (Mike)
29. "A Little Bit of Rain," written and performed by Fred Neil (Mike)
30. "Trouble Again," written and performed by Karla Bonoff (Patti)
31. "R.O.C.K. in the U.S.A.," by John Mellencamp (Mike)
32. "Five O'Clock World," —written by Allen Reynolds and sung by The Vogues (Mike)
33. "What's Forever For," written by Rafe Van Hoy and popularized by country artist Michael Martin Murphey (Mike).
34. "Summertime Blues," by Eddie Cochran (Mike)
35. Medley: "You're No Good"/"She's Not There," as sung by Linda Ronstadt/The Zombies (Patti/Mike)
36. "In the Midnight Hour," by Wilson Pickett and Steve Cropper (Mike)
37. "Do You Love Me," written by Berry Gordy, Jr., and recorded by The Contours (Patti)
38. Medley: "Hit the Road, Jack," "What'd I Say," and "Twist and Shout" "Hit the Road Jack" and "What'd I Say" were both written by Ray Charles. Phil Medley and Bert Berns wrote twist and Shout, which was first popularized by the Isley Brothers and later by the Beatles (Patti).

Kaiser Permanente Dance (Cancelled)

After the April Fool's Day party, there was nothing in the near future to prepare for, so we took a few weeks off. It was a strange time. Our guests had given the April Fool's Day party such rave reviews that it seemed like our enthusiasm for the band might return, but when band practices resumed, it was the same dreary mixture of malaise and melancholy that had infected our practices since Mike's announcement.

But despite how we felt, we had a gig to prepare for, and if we were anything at that point in our musical careers, we were professionals. So we practiced. But three or four Wednesdays later, Les—who worked for Kaiser—told us that Kaiser was thinking about cancelling both the medical meeting and the party because they were so close to the holidays. We received the news quietly but kept on practicing. But the following Wednesday, Les announced that Kaiser had decided to cancel both events, and at that point our future was a question mark.

Bart Says It All

Following news of the cancellation, a feeling of indecision filled the practice room. With nothing to prepare for, we looked at one another, hoping that someone would step up and tell us what to do. Then Bart cleared his throat and spoke.

He said that although he had been dreading this moment, he thought it was time to talk about the band's future. He said that for the last few months, he and Patti had felt that something that the band once had was missing. But he wouldn't presume that we all felt the same way, and if anyone felt differently they should say so. He paused and looked around the room, but no one said a word.

Bart continued. He said that in the past when he heard that some popular band had broken up, he often wondered why a group that had been successful would suddenly say to hell with it and quit. But after being in a few bands, he thought he knew why that happened. The reason, he said, had to do with the nature of bands. Bands required people with differing sets of expectations to function as a unit, and the glue that held them together was the fun that they had playing together. And even though a band may have achieved various measures of success—and may still be achieving them—once they stopped having fun, in most instances they were done.

He went on to say that from the very beginning, we had no illusions about becoming a great band; our only goal was to enjoy ourselves. But in the process of doing this, we had gone from playing house parties before a handful of people to playing for hundreds of people at some of the best venues in the state. We had achieved what many bands far more talented than ours would never achieve. But maybe it was time to look back with pride on what we had accomplished and call it a day. And although he and Patti would be happy to listen to arguments to the contrary, that would be their recommendation.

But further discussion wasn't necessary. Bart had said it well. There was nothing to argue about and very little left to say—a comment here and there, really nothing of importance—and it was over. The Lovehandles had played their final gig.

CHAPTER 17: THE BEAT GOES ON

Bart and Patti left, but the rest of the band continued to meet in Les's basement. Although our band practices felt strained and purposeless, none of us were ready to give them up. Then Hoggard left, and the three of us—Mike, Les, and I—soldiered on until one night when Tom called us to say that he was putting together another band, there were a bunch of new musicians playing in his basement, it was a lot of fun, and we should join them. We left immediately.

When we arrived, Hoggard's basement was filled with new faces. Weeks before, when Tom had put out the word that he was forming another band, the news had spread like wildfire throughout the medical community, and there was no shortage of singers and players who had come to his home hoping to land a spot in the new band. Although I knew many of these people from work, I would never have guessed that they were also musicians. But Hoggard, with his exceptional people skills, had discovered them and invited them to try out for the band.

The most exciting musician, and the person that Hoggard was building his new band around, was David Winchester, a urologist who sometimes referred to himself as "the tip-top dick doc." Winchester was blond, charismatic, and the best rock-and-roll lead guitarist I've ever played with. He was also a competent vocalist, and two young women, one a nurse and the other an office manager, were already singing backup for him.

But with the exception of Winchester and the ladies, the other spots in the new band were up for grabs. Besides Mike, Les, and me, some of the other musicians competing for a place in the band were the CEO of the local medical society who played rhythm and bass guitar, an orthopedic surgeon who played the drums, and a number of medical people who played keyboards.

THE LOVEHANDLES

For most of us, those nights at Hoggard's were great fun. One set of musicians would begin playing, and after a few songs they would step down so that others could play. But in addition to the pleasure of playing music with other people and getting to know them in a new and different way, these gatherings were auditions. The music Winchester played was pure, hard-driving rock and roll, and sometimes musicians who preferred another musical style or couldn't play well enough to keep up with the band would voluntarily eliminate themselves from consideration. But more often Hoggard would have to inform a hopeful musician that he or she wasn't quite what they were looking for, thank them for coming, and say that he'd see them at work.

We practiced in Hoggard's basement for several weeks before the new band had been chosen and was ready to perform publicly. All four of us—Tom, Mike, Les, and I—made the cut. Initially, Mike had been tried in Winchester's backup chorus, but he was moved to rhythm guitar when Winchester gave the last backup spot to Murray, his children's nanny. The band's final lineup was Winchester on vocals and lead guitar; Mike and Tom on rhythm guitars; Rob Delf (the CEO of the local medical society) on bass; Les on keyboards; Lynn Marie, Michelle, and Murray on backup vocals; and me on the drums.

The band played three or four big, attractive venues, including the new Portland Convention Center, before Winchester decided he wanted his own band, and took the three backup singers and Rob Delf, and brought in an outside drummer.

The rest of us were cut. I had absolutely no hard feelings about losing my place in Winchester's band; He needed a better drummer, and I understood that. Nor were Mike, Tom, or Les upset by not making it into his band. What Mike really wanted was to sing, and his musical preferences leaned more toward folk-rock than they did Winchester's all-out style of rock and roll. Les said that he was ready to take a break from bands and took his keyboard home. And Tom, who was always more interested in putting another band together than playing in it, wished Winchester well.

After that, Winchester's band, Cheap Talk and Lies, enjoyed a brief but wildly successful career before blowing apart amid various forms of excess and threats of legal action—but it was great fun while it lasted.

To our good fortune, the end of Winchester's band freed Rob Delf to play with Tom, Mike, and me, as well as with East Portland Neurology Clinic's newest neurologist, Dr. Howard Taylor. Since we had all been in bands before, we named ourselves Reflux to signify that we were back again. Then when we learned that a band by the same name already existed, we added a capital "X" to the end of our name. Although RefluxX would eventually play several gigs, our greatest delight was just getting together once a week and playing for the fun of it.

One of Howard Taylor's many contributions to the band was that he wrote original music. In fact, Howard was so prolific and made songwriting look so easy that soon Mike was writing his own music, too. Surprisingly, many of their creations were gems, and our performances always featured a few of their songs. Howard and Mike's best original work included the songs "Hysteria," "Slug Killer," "Time Is a Bomb," "I'm an Asshole," "Doctor, Doctor," "45th Parallel," and "Octavia."

Eventually Tom became so busy with other projects that he left the band. Although we had always felt obligated to give Tom a hard time and did so consistently, over the years he had been a good friend, a wonderful band mate, and extremely generous in allowing us the use of his various basements. But now we were on our own and needed to find another place to practice.

We played for a while at our house until Caroline and some of the neighbors complained and we were asked to leave. Since none of the other band members had space for us in their homes, I called John Chassaing of Showcase Music and Sound and asked if he knew of some place in town where we could rent a practice room. John said that there was a building in southeast Portland called Suburbia that rented rehearsal spaces and suggested that I look there. I thanked him, called Suburbia, and went to look at their practice rooms. It was love at first sight, and I rented a room on the spot. Room No. 20 would be our home until the band's demise some ten to fifteen years later.

THE LOVEHANDLES

Suburbia was a very special place. On Monday night—our new practice night—we would climb the long flight of stairs beside the conveyer belt that was there to carry equipment between the two floors and continue down the hall to our friendly, often filthy practice room. Along the way we would pass rooms where different musical styles— blues, pop, soul, heavy metal, death metal, and Christian rock—were spilling out into the hallway. At the top of the stairs there was even a room occupied by an all-girl punk band named Gina Lotrimin after Gyne-Lotrimin—the preferred treatment for vaginal yeast infections. Although Suburbia's bathrooms were either in poor repair, filthy, or both, they redeemed themselves by having some of the best graffiti in the city on their walls.

Within the building there were between thirty and forty rooms, most of which were always rented. The bands were all friendly with one another, and though we were between thirty and fifty years older than the other musicians, they appreciated the fact that we were still at it.

Then Mike became concerned about his hearing and left the band, and when our original six-man lineup was down to just Rob, Howard, and me, I asked Tom Hoggard's son-in-law, Warren Dexter, to join us. That was an excellent decision. Warren was a wild man, but he was another one of those magical creatures that we referred to as "real musicians," and who were always so much fun to play with. In addition, Warren was a good teacher, and kept on me until I could produce a strong, steady beat. I also got pretty good at playing fills, but I was never able to perform an extended solo. But according to Meat Loaf, "two outta three ain't bad," and I respect his opinion.

Of all the people I've met through music, Rob Delf was one of my favorites. And in my growing roster of friends who have died, I probably miss Rob as much as anyone. As I mentioned earlier, Rob was the CEO of a medical organization called the Multnomah County Medical Society, which later became the Medical Society of Metropolitan Portland. Rob was a bright, funny guy who over the years had done so many wonderful things for the medical society that I was shocked to hear that he had been "let go" for inappropriate behavior. Although this amounted to nothing more than singing to his employees, it was enough to earn him a pink slip. Shortly after that, a medical evaluation revealed that he was in the early stages of dementia. Although Rob grumbled about the loss of his job and railed against no longer being allowed to ride his motorcycle, he continued playing with the band. In the bars where he and I would eat and drink prior to band practice—Boche's, the Madison, and the Ladd Taphouse—Rob would stroll among the tables telling stories, singing songs, and reciting rhymes to the women. Although this always embarrassed me, the ladies loved Rob's attention, and bought him drinks and sometimes even dinner. Through the first few years of his illness, Rob's songs and poetry varied and were often interesting and clever, but as the dementia progressed, his message was reduced to:

> Women are good, good, good, good
> Best, best, best, best,
> Yes, yes, yes, yes, yes!

His bass playing, too, deteriorated until he was doing no more than hammering the strings with loud, percussive strums, but we would let him pick the tempo and then play along, creating music around his beat. After band practice we always complimented his playing, thanked him for coming, and asked him to please come back the following week. He was still Rob, and it was important that he be there.

Then one Monday night I went to his house to get him, and he was in bed, his son, Jason, sitting beside him. For the first time in his life, Rob had no interest in going to band practice.

Although I hoped that he might rally and make one more appearance, he never came to band practice after that. When I visited him, he appeared comfortable, even serene, but he didn't recognize me, and he wouldn't talk. He died peacefully at home a few weeks after my last visit.

But Rob would never let me get away with saying that he had "died." In Rob's personal cosmology, no one ever died. They just "transitioned to a different zone of reality," which was where his third and favorite wife, Troby, and his middle son, Eric, would be waiting for him.

Howard, Warren, and I played together until 2016, when the band held its final practice. It had been another good run.

CHAPTER 18: EPILOGUE

Patti

Shortly after the Lovehandles broke up, Patti returned to school to earn her bachelor's degree. Working full-time as a dental hygienist, she attended Concordia College nights and weekends and graduated with a degree in management and communications in June of 1991, the same month that her daughter, Amy, graduated from college.

Oregon laws had changed to allow dental hygienists to become independent practitioners, and Patti wanted to start her own business. To that end, she had gotten a business license, found some office space, and had begun looking for a dentist to sponsor her.

But Bart was not convinced that starting a new business was her best option.

"Patti, if you do this," he argued, "you'll want to be successful, and it'll consume you—not just time-wise, but physically. And at our age, is that really what you want to do?"

"Okay, Mr. Wiseguy," she had answered, "so what do you think I should do?"

And Bart said, "For the first time in your life, you have time to do some of the things that you've always wanted to do, and if you start this business, you won't be able to do them. Besides that, it will take a few years for your business to become profitable, and by then you'll be old enough to retire. And it's unnecessary. We've saved enough that you don't need to work."

But Patti was skeptical. Life had taught her never to depend on men for money, and the thought of not working brought back too many unpleasant memories. But she continued to think about it until finally, in the summer of 1992, just as she and Bart were leaving for a cruise to Alaska, Patti called her boss and told him that she was going to retire.

She began her retirement by working one day a week at the Audubon Society as a volunteer. Then after completing the required training, she became certified in wildlife rehabilitation, treating sick or injured animals—squirrels, minks, and birds of every kind—and preparing them to reenter their natural habitats. In addition to working at the Audubon Society, their home was always full of critters that Patti was caring for, either for the Society or on her own.

Patti earned a name for herself in wildlife rehabilitation. She wrote a monograph on the rehabilitation of squirrels, supplementing it with a video that she had filmed herself. She also became an expert in rehabilitating hummingbirds and got calls from all over the country seeking her advice.

The first hummingbird that she cared for was no bigger than a thimble. It had injured itself by running into a window, and Patti took it home, put it on a heating pad, and injected it hourly with minute quantities of fluids and nutrients. It made a full recovery. In fact, of all the hummingbirds that Patti treated, Bart knew of only one that didn't get better under her care.

Then one night as Patti and Bart were getting ready for bed, there was a knock on the door, and they opened it to find a young man standing on the front porch with an owl in his arms. The man said that he and his wife saw the owl fall out of a tree and he was there so that Patti could treat it. Bart took one look at the owl and said, "Patti, this owl is dead," but Patti shot back "No, it's not," and rushed the owl to the bedroom, put it on a heating pad, and began treating it with subcutaneous injections of steroids and saline. To Bart's amazement, the owl woke up. Patti cared for the owl until it was fully recovered, then took it to Tryon Creek State Park and released it.

Because their house was usually filled with animals in various stages of recovery, it was often difficult for Patti and Bart to leave home. So Patti built a collapsible cage so that she could bring the animals with them when they went to Black Butte Ranch or some other nearby location.

In the 1980s, she began feeding raccoons on their back deck. At first only a few showed up, but as their numbers increased, Patti realized that feeding them had been a mistake. But even when she stopped, the raccoons kept coming. Then Patti began trapping them and taking them to the end of the block and releasing them. But that didn't stop them either. Then she found a company that would relocate each raccoon she trapped for forty dollars, but after spending over four hundred dollars, she began to suspect that there was some other reason for their continued appearance.

The reason was that an elderly couple, Dean and Jenny, friends of theirs who lived across the street, were putting out bags of dog food for the raccoons to eat. That was a problem, for as long as the raccoons were being fed, they wouldn't leave the neighborhood. But try as they might, Patti and Bart were unable to convince the couple to stop feeding them. Then in 2004, Dean and Jenny died within months of each other, and the raccoons finally left the neighborhood.

Patti continued working for the Audubon Society, but she became increasingly frustrated with how the Society was running their care center. Although there were protocols in place for the volunteers to follow, the Society had become inconsistent in enforcing them.

The final straw was a mink. Patti had been treating minks at home and returning them to the wild on her own, but when the Society insisted that she bring the minks back to the care center for them to treat and release, Patti acquiesced. Then one day an untrained volunteer was bitten by a mink, and the animal was euthanized. This infuriated Patti. If the volunteer had been properly supervised, that would never have happened. Because of the Society's carelessness, an innocent animal had been killed. So after working for the Audubon Society for fifteen years, Patti resigned.

Patti continued caring for birds at their home, but in 2008, a year before Bart was planning to retire, she stopped.

Although Mike's request that she stop singing with him had hurt her deeply, music was too important to Patti to give it up. In a little room that Patti called her "music room," she kept her guitar, her keyboard, a karaoke machine, and her sheet music, and she continued making music. Then when Bart retired, thinking that they could now play together again, she had bought him a bass, but because of the arthritis in his hands he could no longer play it.

Patti loved to entertain, and during the holidays she, Bart, and several of their friends would get together while Patti provided the entertainment. Over time, her impromptu performances became scripted performances, and their size and complexity increased. Six years before her death, Patti composed an elaborate musical comedy for their New Year's Eve party with parts for seven or eight people, costumes, and original music. On the day of the performance, a large multicolored globe hung from the ceiling to provide psychedelic lighting while the actors read their lines, sang their songs, and changed in and out of their costumes. Supplying the music were Patti on guitar and keyboards, Bart on saxophone, and Patti's friend Deb Summer on cello. It was great fun and a big hit with everyone.

Both Patti and Bart loved to sail and took over thirty sailing vacations, most of them to the San Juan and Gulf Islands. Other sailing trips were to Tonga, Bora Bora, Raiatea, and Le Taha'a Island in the South Pacific and to the British Virgin Islands, St. Lucia, and Grenada in the Caribbean.

They also took cruises to the Greek islands, Alaska, the Galapagos Islands, and Antarctica, and a crewed sailing trip to St. Martins, St. Barts, St. Eustace, and Nevis in the Caribbean.

Other adventures included a tent safari in Africa and a two-week stay at Camp Denali in Alaska.

Patti was also an accomplished photographer and brought a camera with her wherever she went. As a result, their home was filled with framed copies of her beautiful outdoor photographs.

In 1994 Patti decided that they needed a vacation home, and the following year she and Bart bought a two-acre piece of land in Black Butte Ranch's East Meadow area. Patti's former husband, David Dunahugh, drew up a design for the house, but Patti didn't like the floor plan and made several changes to David's design before she was satisfied. Construction of their home was completed in 1997. In addition to altering the floor plan, Patti chose all the colors, the furnishings, and the decorations, and their Black Butte home became a gathering spot for Bart, Patti, and their many friends.

Although Patti was never close to her older brother, George, she remained close to her mother, Marian, her sister, Suzy, and her brother, David.

Patti's mother was able to support herself and stayed in Cedar Rapids until she was ninety, when Bart and Patti brought her to Portland. Marian enjoyed a few good years in an assisted living facility before a hip problem forced her into a nursing home, where she died a year later in 2008 at the age of ninety-five.

Suzy had been in an unhappy marriage, but after her divorce she had gone back to school, earned a master's degree in psychology, and done very well for herself. Every Saturday morning, she and Patti would talk on the phone for hours. It was one of the high points of Patti's week, and when Suzy died of lymphoma at the age of fifty-eight, Patti was devastated.

Then when David died of multiple myeloma, three of the most important people in Patti's life were gone.

But Patti was never one to sit around and feel sorry for herself. Although these were terrible losses, Patti pulled herself together and resumed her busy life.

Tom

In 1982, Tom became reacquainted with Dr. Mary Burry, a woman he first met in medical school when they were married to other people. But now that both were single, they discovered that they shared a passion for adventure, and made plans for a white-water rafting trip down the Apurimac River in Peru. But as the date of their adventure approached and their feelings for one another grew stronger, they decided to marry and make the trip their honeymoon. The trip was exciting, and they followed it with more white-water rafting, kayaking, scuba diving, sailing, and skiing, often in far-flung locations.

Then Mary had an idea: why not combine medicine with adventure by volunteering for medical missions in war-torn or disaster-stricken countries? Tom approved of the idea, and in 1992 they went to Somalia on their first medical mission. It was a life-changing experience.

As a result of Somalia's civil war, as many as forty thousand refugees had gathered at an area near the northern border of Kenya. Although water was available there, Somalia had been through a seven-year drought, and starvation was rampant.

Tom and Mary's accommodations in nearby Wajir were rough. They slept in a local brothel, the heat was oppressive, the toilets were filthy, and the bathing facilities were barely adequate.

Their medical team consisted of seven healthcare providers, an equal number of translators, and a pharmacist. Clinics were held outdoors, either under a tree or in a makeshift shelter, and people waited in endless lines to see them. Although their patients could be sick with anything, nearly all of the women and children were suffering from starvation and malnutrition, often dying before they could be seen.

This was in part due to Somalia's strongly patriarchal society in which the men ate first, while the women and children got whatever was left. Accordingly, the men crowded to the front of the line on the first day of the clinic, demanding preferential treatment. That night the medical team held a meeting and decided that the clinics would be for the women and children only, and if they wanted to wait, the men could be seen at the end of the day. Grudgingly, the men accepted the new arrangement.

Although it was an uphill battle, Tom and Mary stayed in Somalia for weeks doing what they could to help. During their time there they saw hundreds of people and saved countless lives, but overall more people died than they were able to save. But the experience, though heartbreaking, was priceless and left them wanting to do more.

Their mission to Somalia was followed by trips to Honduras in the

EPILOGUE

wake of Hurricane Mitch, and a year later to Albania to treat refugees of the civil war and genocide in Kosovo. In 2000 they traveled to Turkey to provide earthquake relief, Mozambique to provide flood relief, and Ethiopia to provide famine relief.

By then it was clear to Tom and Mary that their effectiveness in dealing with these disasters would be enhanced if they had a better knowledge of tropical medicine, and in 2001 they enrolled in an intensive four-and-a-half-month course in tropical medicine at the London School of Hygiene and Tropical Medicine. They followed that with a two-week practicum in tropical medicine in Gambia, and after that, they took refresher courses whenever possible.

They finished 2001 with trips to Vietnam, Afghanistan, and Zimbabwe, and in 2003, they visited Iraq and Papua New Guinea. Tom and Mary consider their four-month stay in Papua New Guinea the strangest and most frightening of all their medical missions. At the London School of Hygiene and Tropical Medicine, they met a surgeon who was working in New Guinea and accepted his invitation to join him there. Initially, they worked at a small Christian hospital in the town of Mambasanda, where Tom performed minor surgery and assisted the surgeon on larger cases while Mary administered the anesthesia. But after a few weeks in Mambasanda, they were flown into the jungles of New Guinea to care for the indigenous population.

The tribes of this region were uneducated, superstitious, and continually at war with one another. Warriors wore loincloths and adorned themselves with war paint and necklaces made of beads, shells, and animal tusks. They pierced their noses with animal bones and carried spears, bows and arrows, and machetes to use against their enemies. The warriors were often former headhunters or the descendants of headhunters, and though the government had forced them to give up the practice of eating their enemies, they had stubbornly held on to all their other traditions.

Their belief system was a frightening mixture of murder and revenge. The tribes believed that when people slept, their spirits left their bodies and perched in trees, from which they could fly down onto

211

their enemies and commit murder. Likewise, the spirits of their enemies could morph into animals or inanimate objects and kill them at any time. When someone in their tribe died, even from natural causes, it was thought to be due to a spell cast by a witch from another tribe, which meant that the warriors from the offended tribe were obligated to find and kill the witch. This cycle of death never ended.

Although the doctors treated the warriors' wounds, amputated their mangled extremities, and put in tubes to drain pus and reinflate their lungs after chest injuries, they were never without the feeling that given the proper circumstances, these people could decide that the doctors were their enemies and turn on them.

One day the tribal elders told Tom and Mary that they were expecting an attack from a larger, more powerful tribe, if not that day then sometime soon. That night their cabin was surrounded by a dozen armed warriors, each holding a fire stick—a tree branch with a burning ember on one end—to illuminate the cabin's perimeter. But when the night passed without an attack, Tom and Mary called for help and were evacuated the next day.

They returned to Mambasanda, resumed their work at the hospital, and completed their mission. But a year after leaving New Guinea, they learned that three of their four medical assistants had been killed in tribal fighting.

Their time in New Guinea was followed by missions to Sri Lanka, New Orleans, the Solomon Islands, Haiti (after an earthquake), Guatemala, Nicaragua, Panama, Haiti (during a cholera epidemic), Belize, Romania, and Guatemala. In December of 2013, following the devastation of Hurricane Yolanda, they performed their final mission in the Philippines.

Tom and Mary took these trips when both were busy practicing medicine at home—Tom in family practice and Mary in neuroradiology. And in addition to his medical practice, Tom was teaching, both at OHSU and abroad, as well as heading up medical organizations, serving on committees, and sitting on boards.

In recognition of his service, Tom was awarded the 1999 Oregon

EPILOGUE

Academy of Family Practice Presidential Citation for Service to Family Practitioners, the 2002 Oregon Academy of Family Practice Award for Oregon Family Doctor of the Year, and the 2004 Medical Teams International Spirit of Life Award. Also in 2004, Tom was voted Portland's Rotarian of the Year and was a finalist for the American Academy of Family Physicians/*Good Housekeeping's* Family Doctor of the Year Award. In 2006 he was *Portland Monthly's* Doctor of the Year, and in 2014 he received the OHSU Alumni Association's Esther Pohl Lovejoy Leadership Award for National and International Leadership.

Not bad for a kid who never graduated from high school.

Bart

In the 1970s, the cost of medical care began increasing rapidly. Although a few segments of the health care industry prospered during this period, most did not, and of those who did not, doctors and patients were among the hardest hit. Doctors' incomes decreased while the price of health insurance increased, leaving both doctors and patients feeling helpless and angry. Bart saw this and wanted to find a system in which the cost of health care was less and both doctors and patients were better off, and he thought that this might be accomplished with a new form of health insurance called "managed care."

Richard M. Nixon was the first mainstream politician to take deliberate steps to change the longstanding not-for-profit American healthcare system to a for-profit model driven by the health insurance industry. In 1973, Congress passed the Health Maintenance Organization Act, which encouraged the rapid growth of health maintenance organizations (HMOs), the first form of managed care. Unlike traditional medical insurance in which subscribers were free to choose their own doctors and hospitals, HMOs restricted their choices. Using doctors and hospitals that had agreed to provide their services at negotiated (and often discounted) rates, primary care physicians directed the members' care. Advocates of managed care believed that tighter control over patient choices would eliminate expensive and unnecessary care, thus making health care more cost-effective.

Pacificare was a health plan founded in 1975 as a nonprofit corporation, and the following year it became a federally qualified HMO. The company was incorporated in 1985 and switched to a for-profit status a year later.

Initially, Pacificare operated solely within California, but eventually it began looking to expand to other states, and in 1984 Bart McMullan's group and three other Portland medical offices became the company's first subsidiary outside of California—and Pacificare of Oregon was born. Although Bart and the other doctors had no idea what they might be getting themselves into, they thought it was worth the risk.

Bart's title at the new organization was "medical director," a job that initially he did on his afternoons off. But the company grew rapidly, and one afternoon in 1989, Dave Hallock, the company's CEO, asked Bart to begin working full-time.

The request came as a complete surprise to Bart, who had never envisioned his work at Pacificare as more than just a part-time project. He asked for time to think about it, and when he presented Dave's proposal to Patti, she was as shocked as he was.

But the more Bart thought about it, the more he thought that working within a health plan had its possibilities. Since he left medical school, the practice of medicine had changed for the worse, and working for Pacificare could be an opportunity to reverse that trend.

To help settle the matter, he and Patti presented Pacificare's offer to the rest of the band. But like Bart, the other doctors in the band were unhappy with what was happening to medicine and thought that he should give it a try. The risk seemed small, and if it didn't work out, he could always go back to practicing medicine.

In July of 1989, Bart became a full-time employee at Pacificare of Oregon, and by 1995 he had become its CEO. But two years later, while he and Patti were on vacation, the corporate office restructured the company so that Oregon, Washington, and California were a single region, and Bart and his management team were fired. It was Bart's introduction to corporate intrigue.

At that point, Bart didn't know if he should look for something else within the health insurance industry or go back to practicing medicine, but by Friday of the same week he had been fired, he was contacted by Blue Cross Blue Shield of Oregon, the state's largest health plan, and by Providence Health Plan, one of the state's largest insurers. Within a month he had received attractive offers from both companies, and he decided to go with Blue Cross Blue Shield.

One of Bart's first duties at Blue Cross Blue Shield was settling a longstanding conflict between two divisions within the company. To that end, he rented a conference room at the Portland Marriott Hotel, and at the morning meeting he introduced himself to his new employees, explained his business philosophy, and stated his expectations for the future. Then in an afternoon meeting with the management teams of the two warring factions, Bart said that their inability to work together was hurting the company and that if their differences were not settled promptly, there would be serious consequences.

Then to show that he was serious, Bart fired a troublesome vice president, and almost overnight the culture within the company changed. By 2003, six years after he first joined Blue Cross Blue Shield, Bart was promoted to company president, a position that he held until he retired in 2009.

Although Bart thought that retiring meant that he was done working, that wasn't the case. Care Oregon, the state's largest Medicaid insurance plan, asked him to be their chairman of the board, and after that the list of organizations that Bart was asked to either lead or advise grew steadily. But in 2015, six years after he'd planned to retire, he had had enough and told Patti, "I've gotta get out of this," and resigned from everything except ZoomCare, a novel neighborhood clinic system that he still found interesting.

THE LOVEHANDLES

So how did Bart change from physician to corporate executive, careers that required very different skills? Although Bart's dad was a businessman, he and his father were not close, and Bart had never paid attention to how his father ran his businesses.

Instead, Bart's business education began in the Navy, where his first job was acting as the medical officer on a nuclear-powered submarine carrying sixteen nuclear missiles. In general, the crews of submarines consisted of young, healthy men who didn't need much medical care, but on board a submarine carrying nuclear weapons, there was one particular issue that required attention. In Bart's words, "People get a little weird when they're locked up in a metal tube for two or three months at a time, and it was my job to keep them from going crazy and firing off the nukes."

But picking out which members of the crew might crack under pressure had become much more challenging since the Navy did away with formal psychological testing for submarine crewmembers six months before. The reason the Navy had done this was because the tests were screening out so many men that the Navy was having trouble filling its crews. So in place of testing, the Navy had adopted several less structured methods of identifying unstable individuals, one of which was called "pinging"—a reference to the Navy's practice of locating dangerous underwater objects, such as torpedoes, using sonar.

Psychological pinging went something like this: when a new crewman was sent to a submarine, he underwent two weeks of friendly, informal questioning about his likes and dislikes, beliefs, and prejudices. But after that, the friendliness disappeared, and he was repeatedly "pinged" to see how he would react when his opinions were challenged.

For example, if Bart—a doctor from the South—were being pinged, he might be told, "You know, people from the South have terrible hygiene," or "Doctors like to think they're so smart, but you're really no smarter than anybody else," just to see how he would react. And if Bart reacted with anger, outrage, or anything stronger he would have been transferred to another boat.

From this practice, Bart learned that after potentially troublesome individuals had been removed from the workforce, people from very different backgrounds and with very different beliefs could work together comfortably and effectively. And for Bart, who had spent most of his life going to school with people whose backgrounds and beliefs were similar to his own, that was a revelation.

Following his assignment on the nuclear sub, Bart became the chief medical officer for a squadron of fifteen World War II-era diesel-powered submarines, where his duties included managing public health issues such as communicable diseases, waste disposal, food storage, and air quality. But because he couldn't oversee each of the submarines directly, he had to depend on the medical corpsmen who were stationed on the other subs.

Here he learned that it was much more effective to suggest ways that a corpsman might handle a given problem than it was to issue a direct order for him to follow. Although a direct order worked in the short term, the resentment that direct orders often caused made it more difficult for Bart and the corpsmen to work together in the future. The secret to effective management, Bart learned, was to work in ways that nurtured relationships and minimized conflict. Influencing behavior with suggestions like, "Have you thought of this?" was far more effective than telling someone what to do.

After Bart left the Navy and entered private practice, he was elected medical director of the eleven-doctor clinic where he worked, and later he was asked to be chairman of Adventist's Department of Medicine, positions that allowed him to further hone his management skills.

By the time that Bart was CEO of Pacificare, he had developed a very clear understanding of what was and what wasn't necessary in order to have an effective organization. He had found that an effective organization didn't need the best and brightest people in the world; it just needed good people. Nor did it need the newest and most advanced technology; it just needed technology that worked. But after good people and adequate technology, there were two things that were absolutely essential to an organization's success. First, it needed a few employees who could keep it out of trouble—or if it got in trouble, get it out. These employees possessed a mixture of experience, intelligence, and common sense that Bart referred to as "the wisdom factor," and a successful organization always had a few wise people. But even with good people, workable technology, and a few wise souls, an organization could not be truly effective until every employee was committed to its success.

Bart's management style was based on a combination of communication and respect. By the time he became CEO of Pacificare, he had adopted a practice that he would continue until his retirement from Blue Cross Blue Shield in 2009. Between 5:00 and 7:00 p.m. of most working days, Bart would open his office to anyone who wanted to come in and talk about any problems that they might be having. Then when major problems arose, they had already learned how to work together and could tackle them more efficiently.

One practice that Bart thought was absolutely essential to a company's success was prompt communication. He believed that every time one employee received a message from another employee—a voice mail, an email, or a message from their secretary—it was important to respond to it by the end of the day. Although it wasn't necessary to answer each message completely that same day, the person who sent the message should at least know that they'd been heard. This was simply a matter of respect, and a person who felt that they had been treated respectfully was much more likely to do what you wanted than one who felt that they had been treated rudely.

Then there was firing. Although firing employees was always unpleasant, it was a necessary part of corporate life. At other companies, firing was often handled by subordinates or done through their human resource departments, but Bart thought this was disrespectful and did all the firing himself.

Since Bart's goal was always cost containment, his most important and often most difficult job was negotiating fees. Although Pacificare was small enough that he could sometimes avoid dealing with people or institutions that he knew would be problematic, Blue Cross Blue Shield was simply too large for Bart to ignore anyone. As a result, contracts with every clinic, hospital, and service provider in the state had to be negotiated and signed.

One year the director of a large medical clinic insisted that his clinic's doctors be paid 20 percent more than what Bart was paying doctors elsewhere in the state. The director had recently been hired and was anxious to show off his negotiating skills.

Although Bart was willing to give the clinic a point or two above his usual rate, 20 percent was out of the question, and when repeated conversations failed to resolve the issue, the clinic director announced that he would not be renewing his clinic's contract with Blue Cross Blue Shield.

The situation was now an emergency. Bart flew to the city where the clinic was located and talked with all the employers who had their company's health care through Blue Cross Blue Shield. He explained that he was having trouble negotiating with the clinic and asked for their patience. But when further negotiations with the clinic failed, Bart went to the local newspaper and told a reporter that the clinic director wanted them to pay the clinic's doctors 20 percent more than what Blue Cross Blue Shield was paying doctors elsewhere in the state, and if that happened, it would be the subscribers who paid the extra cost. The next day, the story appeared on the paper's front page.

A few weeks later, Bart received a call from the clinic director who said that he'd changed his mind and would be willing to take Bart's last offer. But Bart's answer was, "You can't have it."

The clinic director was stunned. "What do you mean, I can't have it?" he shouted.

"Just what I said," Bart told him. "You can't have it because you've caused us harm. I've spent days dealing with this problem, and it's created uncertainty among our subscribers and their employers. I'll pay you two dollars less than my last offer, and I'll need a three-year contract."

The director was dumbfounded. "But you can't do that," he sputtered, "it's illegal."

"No," Bart answered calmly, "it's not illegal. It's a negotiation. And we'll need your answer in two days."

Two days later, the clinic director called to accept Bart's offer.

A similar problem developed between Blue Cross Blue Shield and one the state's largest healthcare delivery systems, which wanted substantially more money for its doctors than Bart was willing to pay. But when negotiations stalled, a meeting to discuss the company's final offer was scheduled at Bart's office.

The stakes were high. This organization was far larger than the clinic he'd gone up against before, and although Bart needed their business, it had to come at a price that he could afford. If he gave in to their damands, word of Bart's capitulation would spread like wildfire, and every provider in the state would be asking for a higher rate.

On the day of their meeting, the health care system's team of accountants and negotiators arrived with stacks of files and pages of calculations. Sitting across from them, Bart and his vice president, Stephanie Dreyfus, had brought nothing.

Then Bart asked them what they wanted to discuss, and was told that they wanted to discuss pricing.

Bart's response to this was that he was sorry, but he and Stephanie were there to discuss an exit strategy.

"An exit strategy?" the negotiator asked.

"Yes, an exit strategy," said Bart, "So that you can do business without us and we can do business without you. We understand your position, and we're sympathetic. Your doctors need more money than we can pay, and we respect that, but in order to end our relationship cleanly we'll need an exit strategy."

The negotiator looked confused.

"But why won't you discuss pricing?" he asked.

"Because we've already done that," Bart answered, "And now all that remains is for us to agree on a date and a method, so we can end our relationship in a civil manner."

Bart's strategy worked, and both sides settled on an acceptable rate.

EPILOGUE

Larry Franks

In 2001, Larry retired from medicine. This was a great loss to me and the rest of the Adventist medical community, but Larry's endless hours at the hospital had kept him from his wife and children long enough, and he wanted to enjoy his family before the kids left home for college and families of their own. In addition to Geoffrey, Larry's son by his first wife, he and Ulrike had four children: Lawrence, Marin, Jordan, and Nathanael.

Their home sat atop a beautiful 60-acre piece of land that we laughingly referred to as "Franks Mountain" but which contained a full working farm complete with a forest, fruit trees, pasture land, cattle, goats, turkeys, geese, ducks, and chickens. Larry had happily settled into the role of suburban farmer.

Then in early 2016 I received a call from Larry.

"Hey, doctor," he said matter-of-factly, "I just wanted to let you know that I've been diagnosed with stomach cancer. A few weeks ago I began noticing that less and less food was making me full, which as you know can be a symptom of linitis plastica, the kind of cancer that infiltrates the wall of the stomach and shrinks it. Last week an upper GI confirmed the diagnosis. But the MD Anderson Cancer Center in Houston has a treatment protocol for linitis plastica, and I'm going there next week. If my cancer is confined to the stomach, they'll put me on six months of chemotherapy then remove my stomach. So we'll see what they say. Just thought I'd let you know."

But Larry's trip to MD Anderson showed that the cancer had spread outside the stomach. Although he was offered chemotherapy, the statistics for treating this particular form of cancer with chemotherapy were not that much different than they were for doing nothing, so Larry decided against it. He'd lived a good life.

In his final months, a small group of friends met him every week or two for lunch, but as his cancer progressed, he was forced to give up

221

food in favor of ice cream, until he couldn't eat even that.

Larry died on July 16, 2016, twelve days after he and Ulrike had finished bringing in the hay.

Andy

When I went to medical school, pharmaceutical companies were always giving us things: books, stethoscopes, medical bags, tuning forks (to test hearing), reflex hammers, and so on. No, it's not allowed today. But one of the gifts that I received was a book called *Syndromes of Mental Retardation*, which had pictures of kids with the various syndromes, the genetics of their diseases, the specific problems they faced, and what happened to them over time. It was a very nice book: hardbound, with color pictures and well-written summaries.

Three months after my son Andy's surgery had brought an end to his seizures, the seizures returned. We went through all the medicines again but without much benefit, and in desperation we called Dr. John Girvin, the neurosurgeon in London, Ontario, who had done Andy's first surgery, and asked what we should do. He suggested another surgery, this time specifically for epilepsy. He was sure that it would make Andy better.

We flew back to Ontario, where Andy had a second surgery, which was followed by a complication that required a third surgery. But when all was said and done, Andy's seizures were no better.

Then it became clear that in addition to seizures, Andy had significant developmental delays, and we began working with speech therapists, occupational therapists, and physical therapists. In addition, we tried any new or novel therapies (as long as they didn't sound too crazy) that we thought might help Andy catch up. Caroline sought play opportunities and playmates to improve Andy's socialization. She looked for babysitters and eventually nannies that could handle a child with Andy's special needs. We invested endless hours and effort on Andy's behalf with few tangible benefits, and though it was frustrating and sad, we pushed on, searching for that one special something that might make Andy a more normal kid.

Throughout all this turmoil, the one question that hung over everything was this: was there some underlying disease responsible for all of Andy's problems? Then we saw another pediatric neurologist who thought that Andy might have one of the diseases in my Syndromes of Mental Retardation book: tuberous sclerosis. Tuberous sclerosis, or TS, was characterized by seizures, benign tumors, developmental delays, and certain physical characteristics, and it fit Andy pretty well.

But when I listened to the neurologist's arguments, I couldn't accept them. For one thing, the tumor that was initially removed from Andy's brain, though benign, was not one of the tumors characteristic of tuberous sclerosis. For another, TS was an inherited condition, and there was no history of anything like it on either side of our family. But the larger, more compelling reason that I rejected the diagnosis of tuberous sclerosis was that emotionally I couldn't accept it. No child of mine was going to have a syndrome.

Then Andy developed another tumor, and when it was removed and examined under the microscope, it was compatible with tuberous sclerosis—and my defenses crumbled. I had no choice but to accept that Andy had tuberous sclerosis.

But accepting the diagnosis turned out to be easier than I expected. Although tuberous sclerosis was often an inherited disease, 65 percent of the time it occurred because of a spontaneous mutation, and therefore a family history wasn't necessary. But the best reason for accepting it was that in his own way, Andy turned out just fine.

He is now thirty-three years old, and although he still has seizures, they are not the problem that they once were. Although his language is limited, he can communicate well enough. He has a little weakness on his left side, but he is mobile and can do everything that he wants to do. And although he cannot live alone, he has a wonderful foster family, and his room is filled with the things he loves. He smiles readily, laughs easily, and is fun to be around. Although he needs care, everybody loves Andy, and you can't beat that.

THE LOVEHANDLES

Me

Since my life after the band was largely taken up with my work as a neurologist, I would like to tell you about neurology. Put briefly, neurology is a medical specialty concerned with the diagnosis and treatment of diseases and conditions affecting the brain, spinal cord, nerves, and muscles. But it is much more than that.

The problems that neurologists care for include several varieties of headache, a number of types of stroke, multiple forms of epilepsy, an assortment of peripheral nerve diseases, multiple sclerosis, Parkinson's disease, tremors and assorted movement disorders, Alzheimer's disease and other dementias, restless leg syndrome, narcolepsy, and various forms of muscular dystrophy. In addition, neurologists must be able to identify certain mental disorders—catatonia, hysteria, malingering, and Munchausen's syndrome—which often look like neurologic disorders but really aren't.

The two things that separate neurologists from other doctors are their ability to perform a neurologic examination and their knowledge of neuroanatomy. Whereas an ordinary physical examination consists of taking the patient's temperature, blood pressure, and pulse; listening to their heart and lungs with a stethoscope; palpating (feeling) their abdomen; examining their genitalia; and doing a rectal exam. A neurologic exam is very different.

Some of the things that may be done in the course of a neurologic examination are:

1. Checking cognition with either a simple test of orientation (time, place, and person), or with the thirty-question "Mini-Mental State Examination."
2. Testing visual acuity and the condition of the visual fields.
3. Looking inside the eyes for papilledema (swelling of the

optic nerve due to increased pressure inside the head) and abnormalities of the retina.

4. Examining the movement of the eyes and checking for nystagmus (an abnormal oscillation of the eyes).

5. Assessing the size, reactivity, and symmetry of the pupils, as well as the presence and symmetry of the corneal reflexes.

6. Testing hearing and sense of smell.

7. Listening for problems with speech, including slurring (dysarthria) or abnormalities of language (aphasia).

8. Observing the symmetry of facial movements, as well as movement of the tongue and soft palate.

9. Testing the extremities for strength and sensation (touch, pain, position sense, and vibratory sense), as well as for dexterity and tone (flaccidity or spasticity).

10. Looking for the presence of tremors, both during movement and at rest.

11. Determining the state (activity and symmetry) of the deep tendon reflexes.

12. Checking for abnormal reflexes (snout reflex, rooting reflex, palmomental reflex, Hoffman's reflex, Babinski's reflex, and so on)

13. Examining for abnormal muscle twitches (fasciculations)

Those are just some of the things that may be part of a neurologic examination. But there are more. In fact, there are many more. In 1950, Dr. Russell DeJong published his classic work *The Neurologic Examination*. Now in its seventh edition, the book is well over a thousand pages long. You get the idea.

The other thing that separates neurologists from other doctors is their knowledge of neuroanatomy. Although pictures of the brain, spinal cord, and nerves may make the nervous system appear solid and homogeneous, the human nervous system is actually made up of 86 billion nerve cells (neurons)—some of them up to three feet long—that travel about the nervous system in clusters called "tracts."

Each individual neurologic function has several tracts devoted to its performance, and each tract travels through the nervous system on its own unique route. Although neurologists don't need to know where every one of those 86 billion neurons goes, they must have a good working knowledge of where most of them go.

This knowledge of neuroanatomy allows neurologists to take what they learned from the neurologic exam, combine it with the information they got from the patient's history, and determine both what the problem is and where within the nervous system it's located. It's like a gigantic jigsaw puzzle.

To learn neurology, I attended the University of Minnesota for three years between 1969 and 1974. During my time there, the University of Minnesota had one of the largest and most prestigious neurology programs in the country, the program run by a short, brilliant despot by the name of Dr. Abraham Bert (A.B.) Baker.

Neurology is considered a minor medical specialty at most teaching institutions, but not at the University of Minnesota. In general, the status of a medical department and the person running it can be inferred from the number of hospital beds that are reserved for that department's use, and between four hospitals in the Minneapolis/St. Paul area, the department of neurology controlled nearly two hundred beds. Besides demonstrating the power of Dr. A.B. Baker, all those beds meant that there would be a wide variety of diseases and conditions for students, interns, and residents to learn from.

Each morning at 9:00 a.m., amid a cloud of Aramis Cologne, Dr. A.B. Baker would arrive at the University Hospital's neurology nursing station to make rounds. He was then in his early sixties and no more than five feet, six inches tall with small, sharp eyes; a bald head; a large nose; and the bearing of a head of state. Encased in a starched white coat with "Chairman, Department of Neurology" stitched on the lapel above his nametag, Dr. Baker was all business: no jokes, no small talk, no bullshit.

Following his arrival, a host of nurses, therapists, medical students, interns, and residents would suddenly materialize and follow the great man from bed to bed on his morning rounds.

When called upon to do so, any one of the students, interns, or residents caring for a particular patient might be asked to present that patient's history, demonstrate any abnormal examination findings, report the results of consultations and tests, recite the patient's differential diagnosis (the list of all possible diagnoses) and then explain why one or two of them were more likely to be the correct diagnosis, deliver the patient's treatment plan, and explain why the patient was better or worse than they'd been the day before.

Understandably, rounds with Dr. Baker could be very stressful. The amount of information that you were expected to know and digest was endless and ever-changing, and needless to say, Dr. Baker did not look kindly on ignorance, misinformation, or mental sloppiness. But for good work, you could be rewarded with a nod, a smile, or a kind word that would have you walking on clouds for the rest of the day.

But regardless of how you fared personally during rounds, listening to Dr. Baker analyze each case was an extraordinary experience. His knowledge, intellect, insight, logic, and common sense would leave you stunned. You had been in the presence of genius.

On Saturday mornings a few medical students, a handful of interns, and the department's fifteen or so neurology residents would crowd into a tiny conference room for that week's "Case Conference." The rules of this game were simple: the chief resident would select a difficult or instructive case from the previous week's patients and present it—a few pieces of information at a time—for Dr. Baker to solve. Along the way Dr. Baker would use the case to test our knowledge and problem-solving abilities.

My first Case Conference began when Dr. Baker asked the chief resident, "Well, Dr. Meyer, what do you have for me today?" and the chief resident answered, "Dr. Baker, I have the case of a sixty-seven-year-old man who presented to the emergency room in a coma."

Dr. Baker went to the blackboard and wrote the words "sixty-seven," male," and "coma," underlined them, and then turned to the audience, his eyes twinkling.

"Coma," he said dismissively, grinning at his little audience. "Well, this won't take long. Dr. Meyer must have tickets for the [University of Minnesota] Gopher football game this afternoon."

Everyone laughed, but Dr. Baker's smile vanished and he turned back to the chief resident. "Did he lose consciousness slowly or suddenly?" he asked.

"Suddenly," Dr. Meyer answered.

Under "coma," Dr. Baker wrote "suddenly" and the word "exam" to the right of it.

"How many Babinski signs did he have—none, one, or two?" he asked. The Babinski sign is an abnormal reflex elicited by stroking the bottom of the foot. Its presence indicates an interruption of the motor pathway on the opposite side of the brain.

"One."

"Which side?"

"Right."

Below the word "exam" Dr. Baker wrote "R Babinski."

"Is he still with us?" Abe asked the resident.

"No, sir," Dr. Meyer answered. "He died that night."

At that point Dr. Baker turned away from the chief resident, nodded his head, and smiled. He would ask no more questions about the case; he knew the diagnosis.

Now it was our turn. He began by asking us how to differentiate the various causes of coma based upon the history and examination findings. Then when that subject was exhausted he moved to the particulars of the present case.

Finally, Dr. Baker turned to the blackboard and wrote, "Diagnosis: left cerebral hemorrhage." Smiling, he asked the chief resident, "Well, Dr. Meyer, how did I do?"

"You did well, sir," said the chief resident. "The autopsy showed that he died of a left cerebral hemorrhage."

"It was a blessing that he died," Dr. Baker then told us parenthetically. "He would have been miserable not being able to communicate."

And that was my introduction to the Baker method. With just four questions, Dr. Baker had arrived at the correct diagnosis—a cerebral hemorrhage—and its location within the left hemisphere. The suddenness of the man's loss of consciousness had indicated a stroke, the right Babinski reflex told him that the problem was in the left hemisphere, and the patient's quick demise pointed to a hemorrhage. And because the left hemisphere also held the centers for speech, Dr. Baker let us know that had the man survived he would have been both unable to speak and to understand the speech of others, and therefore his death was a blessing.

On another Saturday morning the case was a fifty-five-year-old woman with dementia, and after writing her age, gender, and the word "dementia" on the board, Dr. Baker turned to me and said, "Dr. Crumpacker, tell us the seven treatable causes of dementia."

I came up with four or five, and an older resident supplied the rest. The complete list was neurosyphilis, hypothyroidism, vitamin B12 deficiency, folic acid deficiency, a falx meningioma (a benign tumor located on the fibrous partition—the falx—between the frontal lobes), bromide intoxication, and normal-pressure hydrocephalus.

At other teaching institutions, discussions of dementia usually began with the most common form of dementia, Alzheimer's disease, followed in descending order by the other, less common dementias. But A.B. Baker didn't want us to remember the dementias as a list of diseases. Since most dementias were progressive and fatal, remembering the ones that were treatable was both easier and vastly more important than being able to regurgitate the entire list. Remembering all the dementias may be an impressive feat, but remembering those that were treatable saved lives.

The Baker method of neurology was based on the principal that a neurologist should be both logical and practical, and in order to make his teaching more memorable, Dr. Baker often condensed them into short, pithy axioms, such as "the seven treatable causes of dementia." He also emphasized that 90 percent of the time a neurologist should be able to arrive at the correct diagnosis using the patient's history and examination findings alone. In other words, in most instances tests weren't necessary. This mindset was particularly important because at the time—the early seventies—good tests of the nervous system were few and far between. The tests that neurologists depend on today—CTs and MRIs——were still years away.

But more than anything, the Baker method was fun, giving neurology a playful, game-like quality; each new patient put you at the blackboard of Dr. Baker's classroom, ready and eager to make the diagnosis and provide the proper treatment.

I loved everything about the practice of neurology. I loved the art and science of the specialty itself, but I also loved the freedom of private practice: having my own office; decorating it the way I wanted; and staffing it with nice, capable people.

Another part of neurology that I loved was dictating letters to the referring physicians. Although communication between referring physicians and specialists in the computer age has devolved into the noisome practice of checking boxes on templates, the now-ancient art of composing medical letters has gone the way of the dinosaurs. Sometimes several pages long, these letters contained the patient's complete history, their examination findings, and the reasoning that led the specialist to their conclusions and recommendations. They were informative, readable, and—for me—a joy to dictate.

But most of all, I loved my patients. Because neurology's lineup of diseases consists largely of treatable but incurable conditions, neurologists form intimate relationships with their patients that often continue for many years. They become your extended family. When I retired in 2013, the hardest thing I had to do was say goodbye to my patients.

So, in assessing my life since the Lovehandles, I would have to say that unlike the other members of the band, I've done little that was groundbreaking or exciting. The only awards I've received were athletic. And though I'm understandably proud of them, I'm proudest of my work as a neurologist, my marriage to Caroline; my son, Andy; my relationships with stepsons Bill and Tim, Tim's family, and my friends. Those have meant the most to me.

Les

Les's life from the demise of the Lovehandles until his own death in 2014 is largely unknown to me. I know that he played piano with the remnants of the band while we were still practicing in his basement, and he played a few gigs with Hoggard's new band, but after that, Les said that he needed a break from bands and he took his keyboard home. Then when Les remarried, it became a matter of Caroline and I choosing between our friendship with Les's first wife, Cheryl, who Caroline had been close to for many years, or striking up a relationship with Les and his new wife, Mary—and we chose Cheryl. After that Les and Mary had a daughter, Malia, whom I've never met but I've heard is a fine young woman.

Les and I were never close, and the only contact that we had after his second marriage came about because of a housekeeper that both our families shared, a wonderful lady by the name of Dorothy Jenkins. When Dorothy's daughter, Barbara, became gravely ill, Les and I ran into each other in her hospital room, and then spent an hour or two in the hospital cafeteria catching up on each other's lives. It was then that I learned that Les was facing a decision with enormous financial implications.

Here I need to state that I have nothing approaching an in-depth knowledge of Les's finances, so what I am about to say is based on my memory of that one conversation, and the rest is purely conjecture. So please take the following few paragraphs with several grains of salt. First, I'll begin with my memory of our conversation.

As I recall, Les told me that when his parents, Evins and Dorothy, died, instead of appointing someone to sell their tangible assets and divide the proceeds between Les, his children, and Larry's daughter, Willow, their will made Les the executor of the estate with the freedom to manage it as he saw fit.

The Lovehandles

The most significant property in the estate was a piece of land in downtown San Luis Obispo, California, that was covered with upscale buildings occupied by high-end businesses. Les was not only the owner of the land, but he was also the owner of the buildings, and because the rent that he was collecting was significant, he chose not to sell.

But then the city of San Luis Obispo threw him a curveball. The city passed a law that required all older buildings, like the ones on Les's property, to be retrofitted to make them earthquake resistant, and that was going to be expensive—very expensive. And as we sat in the hospital cafeteria catching up with one another, the question that Les was trying to answer was whether he should sell the property at a price considerably less than its value and let the new owners pay for the required changes, or pay for the retrofitting himself and continue collecting the rent. As we talked, Les had not yet made a decision, but he was leaning toward financing the retrofitting himself, and that was apparently what he did.

Now for the conjecture part. The loans that Les and Mary took to pay for the retrofitting would have been huge and most likely would have strained their financial resources, a situation that would have been made worse by Les's death when Mary no longer had the benefit of his income. And if that, or anything resembling it, is what happened, my sympathies are with everyone concerned.

In 2014, Les was in San Luis Obispo on business when he died suddenly in his motel room. His daughter, Malia, who was attending California Polytechnic State University in San Luis Obispo, was the one who found him.

The deaths of Evins and Dorothy were equally tragic. In the wake of Les and Cheryl's divorce and Larry's initial disappearance—but probably unrelated to both—Evins became depressed. His depression was refractory to treatment, and after years of institutional care, he died in a nursing home in 1997. Dorothy, fared no better. Although her problem was heart disease instead of depression, it was also progressive and untreatable, and she died in 2002.

Then there was Larry. As you may recall, Larry Naman's mental illness and his homelessness were very upsetting to his parents, who became obsessed with trying to find him but were never successful. But in 1997, Larry resurfaced. While living in Arizona, he shot Maricopa County Supervisor Mary Rose Wilcox in the butt for voting in favor of a sales tax to pay for the construction of a new baseball stadium for the Arizona Diamondbacks. Had he accepted legal counsel, he would have been found innocent due to mental illness, but Larry chose to defend himself and was convicted of attempted first-degree murder. Although he was sentenced to fifteen years in prison, Larry was a model prisoner and was released from prison in 2010 after serving twelve years. But following his release, Larry disappeared again; and since then, all attempts by his daughter, Willow, to find him have been unsuccessful.

But on January 23, 2019, Larry Naman attended a Phoenix City Council meeting to protest the council's proposed funding of the city's professional basketball team's arena without a vote of the people. He said that doing so would be a "bloody act of violence against the public." After the meeting, Larry was questioned about his shooting of Rose Wilcox in 1997, and when he expressed no remorse, Larry was barred from entering all Phoenix city buildings in the future. I'm afraid that this will not be the last time we hear about Larry.

Mike

You may recall from Mike's biography that his career path wound through pre-med, psychology, statistics, computer science, counseling, and psychometry before arriving quite unexpectedly at the brand-new field of health care analytics. His first job in that field was with a with a company called the Superior California Professional Standards Review Organization. The work involved reviewing the hospital stays of Medicare patients to see where money could be saved, and to his surprise, Mike loved it.

THE LOVEHANDLES

Mike worked ten years for various professional review organizations. When he began, the work was unregulated and creative, but over time Medicare imposed so many restrictions on how the work was done that the creative element disappeared, and in 1987 Mike quit and became an independent contractor doing database development and consulting. But in 1989, while working on a project for the Providence Health Plan, one of the state's largest insurers, Mike was offered a job as their director of health care analytics, and accepted.

Much of the work that Mike did during his fifteen years at Providence was groundbreaking. His department gathered and analyzed data on subjects as diverse as rating physician efficiency and quality, and detecting fraud and waste by medical providers.

But in 2014, another opportunity appeared. At Providence, Mike's department analyzed data from their own health plan subscribers, who made up about 10 percent of the state's population. But there was another organization in Portland called the Oregon Health Care Quality Corporation (Q-Corp) that had access to data from every health insurance plan in the state—or about 95 percent of the state's population—and they had offered Mike a job.

For Mike, who was trying to develop the most incisive metrics that he could, a larger database would mean greater accuracy, and working for Q-Corp was just too attractive to pass up.

Q-Corp was an interesting company. It was one of fifteen organizations scattered across the country that had been created by the Robert Wood Johnson Foundation—the nation's largest public health philanthropic organization—for the purpose of finding innovative ways of improving health care quality. Each organization was independent and free to work on whatever projects their board of directors thought were important.

Q-Corp's board wanted their organization to analyze data from all of the state's insurance companies. To accomplish this, each month the insurance companies were to submit their data to a single repository that would send it on to Q-Corp, where Mike and his team would analyze the data and develop metrics that insurance companies could use to improve their products and subscribers could use to select their health plans, doctors, and hospitals. On paper it sounded perfect.

But after working at Q-Corp for two years, Mike resigned in frustration. The data that he was supposed to be getting from the insurance companies was frequently incomplete or late, which meant that answers to the questions he was asking could be delayed for months and sometimes years, and as a result, they were often outdated by the time they were published. The other factor in Mike's departure was that he was constantly being asked by other organizations to work on projects that sounded more interesting than those he was working on at Q-Corp. So once again Mike became an independent contractor, a job that he is still enjoying today.

Like his professional career, Mike's music has taken some interesting twists and turns. After leaving RefluxX because of concerns about his hearing, Mike joined a forty-member community choir with the unusual name of PDX Vox—"PDX," being the airport code for Portland, and "vox" being the Latin word for "voice." The group's director was fond of creating choral arrangements for popular music. At one concert that I attended, the choir sang Paul Simon's "Diamonds on the Soles of Her Shoes," the American folk song "Shenandoah," and The Police's "Every Breath You Take," and did so beautifully.

PDX Vox gave two major public concerts each year and made numerous appearances at nursing homes, neighborhood festivals, street fairs, and other community events. On one occasion, they sang Leonard Cohen's "Hallelujah" at the memorial service for a popular judge in the judge's courthouse. It had been his favorite piece of music.

But after four years with PDX Vox, Mike and six other members left to form a smaller a cappella group they named the Stumptown Seven. Stumptown was one of Portland's nicknames from the 1800s when trees were cut down to accommodate the city's growth, their stumps left standing; and of course, six plus one is seven.

Like PDX Vox, the group performed at churches, retirement homes, festivals, and street fairs, as well as the Community Music Center in southeast Portland. But after being together for several years, other aspects of their lives intervened, and the group stopped performing.

A few years ago, Portland's Bureau of Parks and Recreation initiated an interesting program called "Build a Band," which encouraged people who wanted to be in a band to fill out an application form listing their age, musical instrument, experience, and musical preferences so that they could be put together with other musicians in a band. The idea captured Mike's imagination, and he was matched with a group of surprisingly compatible musicians. Their folk-rock outfit, Dysband, performed together for six years.

Currently, Mike and his daughter, Lori, who is also a singer, give yearly Christmas performances at Sky Lakes Hospital in Klamath Falls. Mike also plays at Artichoke Music's Thursday Night Open Mic and its Saturday Morning Song Circle, and he still plays house parties, birthdays, and weddings—basically wherever he is invited to play. His telephone number is available on request.

In addition to his work and his musical career, Mike has somehow found time to participate in various athletic events around the state. He has completed four marathons and has ridden his bike in seven Cycle Oregons, six Chilly Hillys, four Tour de Blasts (on Mount Saint Helens), and what he describes as "too many" century (hundred-mile) bike rides. Mike's son, Scott, who works for the Microsoft Corporation in Redmond, Washington, is also an avid cyclist, and has accompanied Mike on several rides.

But perhaps Mike's favorite pastime is spending time with his two granddaughters, Lily and Kaylee, who live in Klamath Falls with their mother, Lori, and their father, Josh. And in case you're wondering, both girls like to sing.

THE END

ACKNOWLEDGMENTS

Although writing this book was a labor of love, it was still a labor. Each of my first three books took about a year to write; this project took two years. Although the story of the Lovehandles is a little longer than each of the other books, the difference in writing time has more to do with its subject matter than its length. Writing biographies turned out to be a surprisingly difficult process, and each history often required several rounds of interviewing, writing, discussing, and rewriting before it was done to my satisfaction and the satisfaction of the person providing it.

But writing those biographies was both rewarding and surprising; rewarding because in the process of getting each person's story I gained a much fuller picture of who that person was and what they had gone through before joining the Lovehandles; surprising because their histories often showed me that these people who I had supposedly known for decades were actually somewhat different than I had previously thought. As a result, the process of writing this book has given me a much better understanding of my friends than I had before.

For this I need to thank everyone who provided me with those biographies. First, many thanks to the remaining band members—Tom Hoggard, Bart McMullan, and Mike Bragg—for telling me their stories, and to Bart McMullan, Ulrike Franks, and Cheryl Woods for telling me about the lives and deaths of Patti Dunahugh, Larry Franks, and Les Naman.

Next I must give a giant shout-out to Bart McMullan for saving all our gigs' set lists and our equipment's instruction manuals. Thanks, Bart, I could never have done this without you.

Then I want to thank my editor, Sarah Currin-Moles for making this account far better than it would have been without her. Once again, it's been a pleasure working with you.

THE LOVEHANDLES

And many thanks to my book designer, Gail Watson, who designed the book's cover and layout, put in the pictures, and oversaw its publication. I'm lucky to have found you.

And finally, I'd like to thank my wife Caroline for giving me the time and the freedom to disappear inside my head for days at a time and write this stuff. Love you.

POSTSCRIPT

On February 9, 2018, Bart McMullan was introduced to Sallie Weissinger by a mutual friend. Originally from New Orleans, Sallie attended Newcomb College of Tulane University and the University of Madrid then went to the University of California, Berkeley, for graduate school. After earning a Master's Degree in Spanish, French, English, and Comparative Literature, she married and left California while her husband was in the service. Six years later they divorced and Sallie returned to California where—after a couple of false starts—she began working for the Federal Reserve Bank of San Francisco, ultimately becoming its Vice President of Human Resources and Public Affairs.

Just as had happened in Bart's two previous marriages, it was music that helped bring them together. After their first meeting, Bart and Sallie corresponded through emails in which the subject quickly became the music they both loved. As it turned out, music was just as important to Sally as it was to Bart.

Bart and Sallie will be married on April 4, 2019, in California. Following the ceremony, Bart's dog, Sulay, and Sallie's two dogs, McGee ("Me and Bobby McGee"), and Tillie ("Till There Was You") will be joining the lucky couple.

One of Sallie's favorite songs is Louisiana-born Johnny Adams' song "There Is Always One More Time," and indeed there is. We wish them many years of love and happiness.

Made in the USA
Middletown, DE
20 May 2019